WHERE DID
ISLAM
COME FROM?

DID IT COME FROM GOD OR FROM CULTURE?

BROTHER K

ANM
publishers

WHERE DID **ISLAM** COME FROM?
Did It Come from God or from Culture?

ISBN: 978-1-946174-08-6 Paperback

Published by:

ANM
publishers

Advancing Native Missions
P.O. Box 5303 • Charlottesville, VA 22905
www.AdvancingNativeMissions.com

For those seeking the truth,
for Muslim brothers and family seeking to know Jesus,
and for my wife, Holly, who has suffered for Christ.

CONTENTS

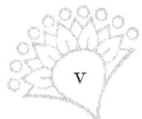

Foreword

The author of this book knows whereof he speaks. His reading and research in Arabic, coupled with his first-hand experience of living in the Middle East, first as a committed Muslim and then as a follower of Jesus Christ, gives him a unique perspective.

His conclusions will be considered controversial by many, and even offensive by some. But the issues he raises deserve a full hearing, and it is difficult to find anyone else raising them. The prophet of Islam, Muhammad, was fully a product of his time and his milieu. The implications of this for his modern followers, especially those who claim most passionately to be following his example, are profound.

In recent years, an odd perspective has arisen where advocates for Islam, both Muslims and non-Muslims, regard any spoken or written criticism of Islam or its prophet as an act of violence. But a fair-minded reader is able to distinguish between acts of violence and critical words. The fair-minded reader will ask of this book whether the facts seem well-established and

the argument coherent. The fair-minded reader will not be disappointed.

One of the strengths of the Western world has been its willingness to look rationally and objectively at truth claims. This cultural value is eroded whenever *ad hominem* attacks or threats of violence are used to intimidate and shut down authentic points of view.

So my wish and prayer is that this book may get a full and fair hearing wherever it goes, and the same for Brother K himself. Godspeed!

Rev. George Ainsworth, M.Div.

A Note
from the Author

I grew up in a Muslim family in the Middle East and I speak Arabic, the language of the Quran. I read many of the Islamic reference books in Arabic and grew up believing a lie. I was taught that before Muhammad started Islam, the people of the Arabian Peninsula, which is called Saudi Arabia today, lived like animals. It was survival of the fittest. The strong killed the weak and the rich enslaved the poor. I was told that they were atheists and worshiped idols. I believed that their economy was built through thievery, raids, and the slavery of women and children. There was no morality in the early Arab communities. Because there was no god and no religion, they had no ethics. The people were uneducated and ignorant. The Islamic historical reference books teach all Muslims these things.

When I accepted Jesus as my Savior, many big questions came to my mind. Where did Islam come

from? Did Islam bring something new? If so, then why did Jesus say, "It is finished," when He was hanging on the cross?

My first ten years as a Christian, I studied this issue to try to discover the facts of Islam. You are now holding the conclusion of my studies in your hands and you will discover that Islam never brought anything new to humanity. On the contrary, Islam has harmed humanity and corrupted and destroyed the image of God for people.

While you're reading this book, you'll discover that Muhammad stole all of the good ethics of the Arabian Peninsula community, rearranged them, and told people that this was a new revelation from Allah. Another thing you will see in this book is that Muhammad had a relationship with both Christians and Jews. Because of these relationships, some of his teachings came from the roots of Christianity and Judaism.

Please consider these questions after reading this book: What new thing did Islam bring to the Arab community? Can you accept Islam to be a religion inspired by God or was this religion born out of the culture and ideas of the Arab community?

Please note that when I say Arab community, Arab tribes or Arabian Peninsula, I am referring to the time before Muhammad, or prior to 530 BC, and the people of Saudi Arabia. Islamic history refers to these people of this time by these names. When I talk about Allah, I am referring to the name used by Arabs for god before

Muhammad. From the beginning of Islam, Muslims refer to their god by this name.

Also, all references are in Arabic because the references are taken from the original Arabic text. Because the Quran is written in Arabic, all historical Islamic books are written in Arabic.

INTRODUCTION

Before Muhammad, the people of the Arabian Peninsula (Saudi Arabia) were educated and governed by ethics and rules in their lives. They lived as tribes, meaning that they lived as families in communities. However, Muslims have described the Arab community during this time period unfairly, claiming it was an ignorant and dark society, drenched in sexuality and idol-worship. They have described it as a tribe that was morally and socially corrupt, lacking culture and urbanization.

When Muhammad introduced the teachings of the Quran, the Arab leaders of that time refused him as a prophet because what he taught was normal for them. The Arabs of that day were great poets and writers. Therefore, he challenged them to create holy verses like his own. The Quran says:

> *Or do they say, "He forged it"? Say, "Bring then a sura like unto it, and call (to your*

aid) anyone you can besides Allah, if it be ye speak the truth!"[1]

Then the Arab leaders, who were a people of science, religion, literature, and poetry, brought him more than one holy verse, so Muhammad said that his Allah challenged them to bring ten holy verses:

Or they may say, "He forged it." Say, "Bring ye then ten suras forged, like unto it, and call (to your aid) whomsoever ye can, other than Allah! – If ye speak the truth!"[2]

If we assume that the Arab tribes of the time were ignorant, weak, and atheistic, Muhammad himself having called these very people infidels, then we need to ask the question, why did Muhammad then through the Quran take many of Islam's rules and laws from these very Arab communities' traditions, customs, and laws, and then give an order to obey these rules or be convicted as an infidel and condemned to death?

Most Islamic historians deliberately hide the benefits and advantages of the Arab tribes in order to corrupt the value of their ethics and rules. At the same time, these historians ignore the reality that they are protecting Islam and its traditions. They are blinded to the fact that Islam absorbed all its rules from the Arab communities.

The goals of this book are to show you the fol-

---

[1] Sura 10:38
[2] Sura 11:13

lowing: (1) Islam inherited all rules from three major ethnic groups during Muhammad's time: the Arabs, Judaism, and false Christianity (also known as Nasraniah). The Quran says:

> *And when our verses are recited to them, they say, "We have heard." If we willed, we could say [something] like this. "This is not but legends of the former peoples."[3]*

Also, (2) the Arabian Peninsula was filled with many different religions, signs, and civilizations. Finally, (3) Muhammad was a normal man, not a prophet inspired by God.

This book will also answer the following questions:

- What was the culture really like?

- Did the people believe and follow any religion or worship in a particular way?

- Did the people worship in sacred places like the Kaaba (the Islamic holy Black Stone) in Mecca (capital city of the Islamic religion, found in Saudi Arabia)?

- Did the people of the Arabian Peninsula become a civilized community with people who learned and gained understanding of the principles and values that would help them improve their society, ultimately reaching the belief in one god, or monotheism?

---

[3] Sura 8:31

PART I

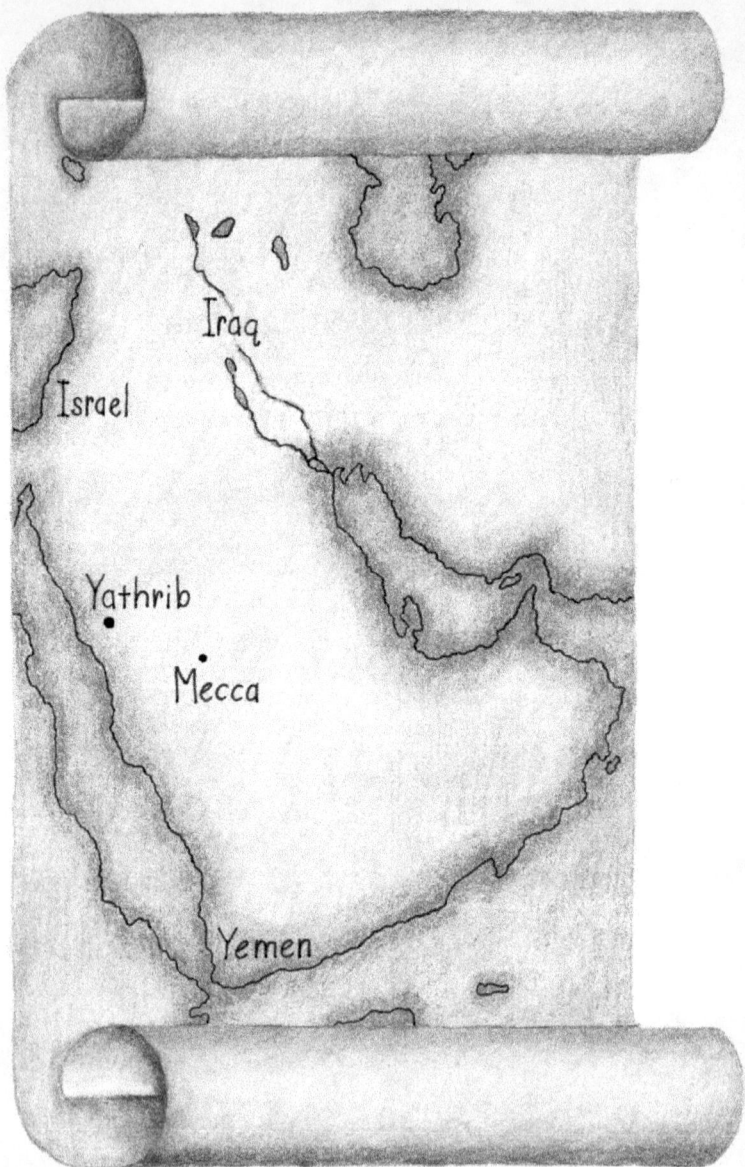

Israel

Iraq

Yathrib

Mecca

Yemen

1
PRE-ISLAMIC ERA

To gain insight into the pre-Islamic era one must understand that it was not a time when people were ignorant, illiterate, or lacked the ability to read and write. Much evidence proves the opposite. During that time, Arabs were some of the most talented poets. Each Arab tribe even had a special poet about whom they boasted. Competitions were held in their large markets and communities to choose the best poem written, which would hang on the walls of the Kaaba in Mecca. They used their poetry like Emro Alqys, al-Farazdak, and Zo Alasbaa Alodwany, among others to condemn other tribes' kings. This proved that Arabs in the pre-Islamic era were creative in their writing, reading, and language. Not only were they creative, but some even learned foreign lan-

guages and frequently traveled to countries such as
Persia, Syria, Egypt, and Yemen for trade.

THE TIME OF IGNORANCE

However, the Islamic historian, al-Alosy, still claimed
that the Arab tribes, although educated, were ignorant
in their knowledge of Allah. He wrote that there were
three types of ignorance: general ignorance, absolute
ignorance, and illiterate ignorance.

General ignorance referred to those who refused
to acknowledge what the Jewish and Christian mes-
sengers said. "And settle in your home; and don't dis-
play yourselves, as in the former days of ignorance."[4]
Referring to the time of Abram, we read: "Those who
disbelieved filled their hearts with rage—the rage of
the days of ignorance."[5]

Absolute ignorance referred to one who remained
in his previous condition, without any faith, and didn't
accept Islam.

Ignorance, therefore, was not indicative of being
illiterate, which is the opposite of science and knowledge. Ignorance in this sense refers to moral ethics,
such as anger, foolishness, bad temper, and rage. This
is the way some Arabs conducted themselves, contra-
dicting patience.

---

[4] Al-Ahzab 33
[5] Al-Fath 26
بلوغ الأرب في معرفة أحوال العرب ج 1ص 14 و 15 و 16

WHY WERE THEY CALLED ARABS?

To understand why the people who lived during the pre-Islamic era in the Arabian Peninsula were referred to as *Arabs,* you must understand the time period it was used.[6]

The term *Arabian* (or *Arab*) was first used in 530 BC in Persian texts written by Akaminah. It meant "the desert between Iraq and the Levant, including the Sinai Peninsula." Then, it was used to refer to the area extending from the Dead Sea to the Gulf of Aqaba in Valley of Arabah, and meant "the drought, the edge of the desert, and the burnt land."

People living in the urban areas are called by the name of their tribe or the place in which they lived. The term *Arab* was used as a general way to refer to those who lived on the Arabian Peninsula. Later it came to be used when the Hebrews came into contact with the Arab tribes who were living in the desert. It is also mentioned in the Old Testament, referring to the Bedouins. Herodotus, the historian, used the term *Arab* in the fifth century BC to refer to all the residents of both the Arabian and Sinai Peninsulas.

European and Greek writers began using the term *Saracens* to indicate the person was "an Arab who professes the religion of Islam." This was derived from the East and means "steal," which is derived from the term

---

تاريخ العرب في عصر الجاهلية . د / سيد عبد [6]
العزيز سالم . ص 13

"thieves" to refer to the Bedouins who were living in the desert.

However, Friedrich Max Müller, writer and professor of ancient history, doubted the authenticity of using the term *Arab* to express the people's nationalism. Because the Arab people were made up of many tribes, but were constantly at war with one another, they were not united as a people.

The Quran is considered the oldest Arabic source and mentions both *Arabic* and *Arab* more than ten times as a way of stating that the language of the Quran is to be Arabic: "We made it an Arabic Quran, so that you may understand."[7]

After a time of extinction, the Arabs went through three stages of social and environmental formation and development. Then, in the centuries to follow, they re-appeared, reproduced, and multiplied according to the stages al-Masudi set up.

First Generation of Arabs

Old Arabs like Aad, Thamoud, and Gerhem lived in the Arabian Peninsula and then perished. The first generation of those who were firmly grounded in Arabism and considered to be innovators, like Qahtanyeen, also perished.[8]

---

[7] Sura 43:3
تاريخ العرب في العصر الجاهلي .د / السيد عبد العزيز سالم
ص 61 ،قصة الحضارة عصر الإيمان . ول ديورانت ص 10

[8] تاريخ العرب في عصر الجاهلية ص 70 ـ فجر الإسلام . ص 15

Next Generation of Arabs

Other Arabs (those who did not perish) came about from Ishmael, who came to Mecca and married a woman from a Yemeni tribe. He spoke Hebrew, then learned to speak Arabic.[9]

ARAB TRIBES

Groups of Arabs who lived together were referred to as "tribes." Socially, the Arab community became stable within their own tribes because of the laws and traditions enacted that governed their relations. Each tribe became the foundation upon which the whole community system was formed. Tribes were in constant conflict, warring with their neighbors all the time, which either led to an alliance or an attack on one another. As a result, the society split into three separate levels: Nobles, Molly, and Slaves.[10]

Nobles

Nobles were the upper-class members of the society, the mainstay of the tribe. The Nobles were the sons of the tribe who were responsible to inform the tribe of an attack and protect them, regardless of whether the tribe was the oppressor or the one being oppressed.

المسعودي ـ مروج الذهب ـ ج 2 ص 56 ـ فجر الإسلام . احمد [9]
أمين . ص 15

مروج الذهب و معادن الجوهر . المسعودي [10]

Molly

Molly were the second-class members who had been cut off from their tribe as a result of committing a shameful or harmful act, which brought shame on the tribe and gave them a bad reputation. Thus, they were dethroned and moved to another tribe, which was considered disloyal to the masters. This dethroning took place in the public markets and forums.

Slaves

Slaves were the third-class members of the society—the majority of the people. Most of them were Ethiopians, captives, and white prisoners of war.

Sheikh

The leader of a tribe was a Sheikh, who was chosen by tribal leaders. The Sheikh would be from a well-known house, famous for his riches and wisdom, and was a great fighter with distinguished qualities and privileges, but he was also entrusted with special commitments. At the onset of Islam, Muhammad set the standard for the Sheikh's special qualifications and commitments. He should be the elder, the noblest, the richest, and have more influence than any other man in his tribe. He would be generous, patient, wise, courageous, and a help to strangers and those who are weak, and he would pay blood money for the poor of his tribe.

Pillaging in ancient times was a custom in which the killer had a right to seize the clothes, weapons, and mount of those who had been killed. This tribal custom eventually moved over, with all its details, to Islamic law. A tribal Sheikh had the right to take a quarter of the family's wealth (after Islam, Muhammad took one-fifth). He was given the privilege of being the first to select a sword, a captive, or a mare before dividing the remaining spoils (after Islam, it was the same in the marriage of Muhammad to Safya). Also, the Sheikh took over the remaining bounty that couldn't be divided.[11]

VIRTUES OF THE ANCIENT ARAB TRIBES

Ancient Arabs formed an alliance called Al-Fudul, which was characterized by patience, defense of the oppressed, fulfillment of promises and vows, and generosity. Muhammad said: "If I had been invited to it after Islam, I would agree." These qualities are what distinguished the Arabs from others.

Generosity

Generosity was one of the characteristics of being a master, boasting in the ability to host strangers and guests. Therefore, Arab tribes would attract strangers at night by lighting a fire and using barking dogs to attract travelers.

تاريخ العرب في عصر الجاهلية ص 415 ـ قصة الحضارة عصر [11]
الإيمان .ول ديوارت ص 11

Generosity also meant helping widows and orphans and is still considered one of the greatest virtues of being an Arab. They were also patient, courageous, and tolerant if asked to help weaker tribes.

Chastity

They were proud of their chastity, which was considered one of the nobler manners. Antar bin Shaddad said he used to close his eyes while a female neighbor was crossing until she disappeared.

Vows

The fulfillment of vows started in Jewish law:

> *"If you make a vow to the LORD your God, you shall not delay fulfilling it, for the LORD your God will surely require it of you, and you will be guilty of sin."*[12]

Arabs adhered to this law and hated treachery.

Hatim al-Tai (a famous Arab poet who belonged to the Tai Arabian tribe) said, "The people advised me to save some money because I spent all mine," and he replied, "Without spending money I would never have been a master!"[13]

---

[12] Deuteronomy 23:21

بلوغ الأرب في معرفة أحوال العرب . الألوسي ج 1 ص [13]
إلى 103 99

MARRIAGE AND DIVORCE

In the Arabian Peninsula, it was illegal for Arabs to marry their mothers, daughters, and aunts. Moreover, some religious parties that existed before Islam forbade some types of marriage, proving the strong influence of Islamic law on people's lives. All of this was approved in the Quran.

Arabs permitted different types of marriage and divorce, which were eventually acknowledged by Muhammad after his prophecy was given.

Marriage of Dowry

An engagement and dowry were determined by the bride's father in *balochi* (or dowry) marriage. This was the preferred marriage among the ancient Arab tribes.

Temporary Marriage

Temporary marriage allowed for a woman to marry for a specified period of time. The man provided a specific dowry after the time period expired and they separated. If the woman gave birth during the period of marriage, the baby remained in the custody of the father.

Captivity Marriage

Captivity marriage was between a warrior and a captive and didn't require a dowry. The master of a female slave had the right to marry her. If any

children were born, they were not allowed to be in the custody of the master, but were considered his slaves. The master might choose to set them free if he so desired.

Divorce

Arabs were permitted to divorce their wives up to three separate times or send them off by giving them money. If the husband died, the wife was required to stay unmarried for a full year to ensure she was not pregnant. Some of these marriage customs stayed in force after Islam was instituted, though some amendments were made. For example, the woman only had to stay unmarried for four months and ten days.[14]

The Arabs living in the pre-Islamic era were influenced by Jewish law and prohibited the types of marriage mentioned in the Bible:

> *"'Cursed be anyone who lies with his father's wife, because he has uncovered his father's nakedness.' And all the people shall say, 'Amen.' 'Cursed be anyone who lies with any kind of animal.' And all the people shall say, 'Amen.' 'Cursed be anyone who lies with his sister, whether the daughter of his father or the daughter of his mother.' And all the people*

*shall say, 'Amen.' 'Cursed be anyone who lies
with his mother-in-law.' And all the people
shall say, 'Amen.'"[15]*

SUMMARY

Now we understand that ignorant in this context
does not mean illiterate, but that rather the pre-Islamic
Arabs were ignorant of the way to god. We also see
that the Arabs had values and ethics before the beginning of Islam. We learned that the leader of the tribes
had advantages over the lay people of the tribes. This
was exactly the same after the introduction of Islam.
Before Islam, Arabs had marriages and laws of marriage, just as they did after Islam.

---

[15] Deuteronomy 27:20-23

2
POLITICS IN THE ARABIAN PENINSULA

The Quraysh community (Mecca) became famous and prospered for many reasons. The Quraysh grew at the expense of the Byzantine and Persian Empires (comprised of Romans, Ghassanid, and Manathira). These empires were failing, while the state of the Quraysh was up and coming.

There are several reasons why the Quraysh grew and the other empires failed. In the first quarter of the sixth century AD, Yemen's agricultural and commercial industries started to collapse. Yemen came under the rule of the Ethiopians and Persians. The poor conditions of the northern kingdoms, Ghassanian and Manathira, made them weak.[16] The political vacuum

جواد العلي المفصل في تاريخ العرب 16

in the area stretched from the southern coast of the Indian Ocean to the northern desert in the Levant. Many commercial paths, which were not safe to travel (except through Mecca), were divided from the northern Yemeni port to Persia in the east and Rome in the north and west, crossing the Palestinian and Egyptian borders. There was war between the Persian and Roman Empires, which caused a great loss in various places and along the roadways throughout the Arabian Peninsula (with the exception of the path to Mecca). The religious persecution against the Jews and Christians by the Persian and Roman Empires played an important role in helping to establish the Quraysh.

On the other hand, the tribes of Hijaz, Mecca, and Yathrib were peacefully enjoying their independence because they were isolated geographically due to the rough terrain.

Because the Quraysh offered safety for a bribe, Mecca was a safe area, and became a major transit station during the time of Qusay ibn Klab (founder of the Quraysh). Then, to avoid sailing through the Red Sea (which was full of islands and had few ports, making navigation extremely dangerous and limited), the Quraysh began buying goods that came through the ports of Yemen to sell and trade with the Nordic countries.

It took one hundred and fifty years for Qusay ibn Klab to establish the Quraysh. He was the first to use religion as a way of joining the Arab tribes through the ritual of pilgrimage, which was accepted by all tribes. He then changed his focus from tribal cohesion to being unified under the domination of the Quraysh. The Qurayshi people became holy, or at least communion with them was holy. They were called "the people of the holy campus," *(Kaaba)* and the elders held a position of dignity and holiness. Ibn Klab ordered them to build their homes inside the campus and said that around the house, "You will be the masters of Arabs forever, and they can't fight you or get you out of your homes." In this way, ibn Klab prepared the way for Muhammad to introduce the Islamic state.[17]

The Al-Malaa government was the authority in Mecca to ensure that the aristocratic businesses were compatible with them on various matters. Only free people over the age of forty or wealthy nobles were allowed to attend the government sessions. The Arabs believed that anyone under forty was not mature. For this reason, Muhammad did not declare himself a prophet until he reached forty years old.

The Meaning of Quraysh

The word *Quraysh* is derived from *al-taqarrush*, which means "gathering after being dispersed." Some people said *al-taqarrush* is related to the profit they gained from trade.

---

17 أبن هشام ج1 ص 63 ـ أبن كثير: البداية والنهاية ج2
ص 187 ـ الإسلاميات . سيد القمني ص30

The Meaning of Mecca

Mecca has three different meanings. The first is related to whistling, as Arabs used to whistle and clap their hands while walking around the Kaaba. The second is related to getting water out by sucking, because it was hard to carry water from the wells. (For this reason, Muhammad promised his followers to have rivers of water in Paradise because the water in Mecca was sparse.) The third is related to being crowded since Mecca was very crowded with people, especially during the times of the pilgrims.[18]

SUMMARY

As you can see here, the Arabian Peninsula had a government system and rules, contrary to what Muslims will teach you today—that the pre-Islamic era was barbaric. We have discovered why Mecca was a strategic city for the Arab tribes.

18 معجم البلدان لياقوت الحموي ج ٥ ص١٨٢ ـ موسوعة
الأديان القديمة . معتقدات اسيوية ص٢٦

3

ECONOMIC, COMMERCIAL, AND CULTURAL BACKGROUND

With the beginning of a new era, the Quraysh formed alliances between the wealthy commercial tribes of Mecca and other commercial tribes on the borders of the Roman and Persian Empires for trade and economic openness. The Quraysh held other alliances with the tribes working inside the Arabian Peninsula, and one with the tribes working inside the Roman and Persian Empires.

It has been said that Arabs in the pre-Islamic era lived in an isolated nation and had no contact with any other nation—they were only in a desert surrounded by the sea. But in reality, they were in contact with those who were similar to them, both physically and morally.

TRADING

Arabs used to travel to Egypt and the Levant for trade—exporting and importing. These trade routes influenced the Arabs greatly as they widened the door to a new livelihood. Some Arabs lived in countries along the trade routes, trading by themselves, while others worked in the service industry as drivers, guards, or guides. In the Book of Songs, it says that Omara bin Alwaleed and Amr bin Alas both were traders and went to Ethiopia.[19]

Moreover, al-Boghdady mentioned that Abd al-Muttalib (Muhammad's grandfather) died in Gaza on the border of Egypt. Also, al-Moghera bin Shoba traveled to Egypt frequently before Islam was established, and Amr bin Alas Abu Sophian traveled many times to Alexandria as a trader of scents and leathers. All of these men were masters and nobles in their nation, and later they used Islam for their own personal gain and led the Islamic army to conquer and occupy the countries of the Middle East.[20]

Due to the animosity between the Romans and the Persians, the people of Mecca were highly established in commerce, and the Romans had become dependent on Mecca for trade in many areas.

Many factors helped influence the development and progression of the Quraysh. Its leaders and nobles

فجر الإسلام . أحمد أمين ص23،24 [19]

هوامش الفتح العربي لمصر. ص7 [20]

used these factors to their benefit, while the same factors led to the collapse of other countries.[21] Financial and political positions were influenced by the change of old trade routes, which led to many temples falling and Mecca prospering.

ELEPHANT MARCH BY KING OF ETHIOPIA[22]

In 569 BC, Abraha, the king of Ethiopia, attacked Mecca with the intent to destroy the Kaaba. However, he was arrogant and did not take into account the difficulty in climate or the rugged roads. He lost all of his army and elephants to diseases like measles and smallpox. Because of his utter destruction, it was easy for the Arab tribes to later believe that the Kaaba was holy. It gave extensive prestige to the Quraysh to call them "the people of Allah." The Quran refers to this story in Sura 1:5.[23]

OKAZ, THE LARGEST QURAYSH MARKET

In order to invest the rewards of switching the trade routes to Mecca, the Quraysh were able to organize some trade markets during specific seasons. Okaz,

---

21 فجر الإسلام . أحمد أمين ص27

22 الروض للسهيلي ج 1 ص73العقاد. طوالع البعثة المحمدية ص145 .الإسلاميات سيد القمني ص27

23 أبن هشام في كتاب الروض للسهيلي ج 1ص 69

which was famous for its commercial, cultural, and religious trading, was forbidden during some months in order to tighten control inside and outside Mecca. The people were only allowed to trade during their pilgrimage (*Hajj*) to the Kaaba.

As a result, a strong economic foundation was formed among the Qurayshi tribes. Leadership links and roles were formed in order to set up trade procedures and construct facilities for shipping and caravan services. The Quraysh built transit stations for foreign convoys and charged them fees to keep the convoys safe. They also charged rental fees for booths at the market. This led to inequality, decoding the old system of how the tribes were linked, and raising the intellectual and economic levels of the Arabs.

INTELLECTUAL LEVEL

The intellectual level of the Arabs in the Arabian Peninsula at this time was high—especially among those who lived in Yemen. Because of the increasing prestige of the Quraysh, all Arabic speaking tribes picked up the dialect of the Quraysh Arabic, and because of this the Quran was written in the Quraysh dialect.[24]

They built mansions and palaces, creating an urban society. One of the most famous was Ghumdan Palace.

تاريخ العرب في العصر الجاهلي ص 104 ـ 111 [24]

They also built castles and cities, showing their knowledge of the sciences that helped preserve their system. They built forts and set up armies. They pursued a functioning scientific water management system, proving their superiority in science and politics.

Al-Raha, Al-Naseeben, Al-Gendsabore, Al-Madina, and Entakia were the most important cities that followed Greek science, medicine, philosophy, architecture, and the belief in using herbs to cure ills.[25]

Entakia

Al-Masudi said in his book that Entakia built a castle with 136 towers and 20,000 rooms. Entakia also built the Church of Mary (one of the wonders of the world).

When al-Walid ibn Abdel Malk came with his Islamic army to conquer this land, he destroyed the church and part of the castle and used the granite from these buildings to build a mosque in Syria. They built fences, forts, and schools, and were interested in material gain as well as religious thought.

Al-Gendsabore

Al-Gendsabore (near Iraq) built a medical school like the one in Alexandria. Students from India and around the world came here to study the use of herbs to heal diseases.

المسيحية و الحضارة العربية . جورج شحاته ص100 -107 [25]

Mecca or Quraysh

Because of the international trading that occurred, the people of Mecca were very wise in their financial dealings. They also were open to many religions, and for this reason there were many idols in the Kaaba. This is why they refused Muhammad when he first presented Islam to them. His logic was weak.

Yathrib (or Medina)

Yathrib (Medina, or *city* as the Jews had called it) was famous for growing grain and grapes and manufacturing and exporting weapons for war and clothing. The presence of non-Arabic groups from Yemen caused this to be an unstable tribal society. Twenty Jewish tribes and Nasraniah caused inner conflicts and conspiracies within the tribes, which weakened the political power (as compared to that of Mecca). Yathrib's focus on agriculture and weapons caused the people of Mecca to be hostile toward them. This led to a tribal conflict—contradiction and competition of interest between them.

The three famous Jewish tribes in Yathrib were Banu al-Qaynuqa, Banu al-Nadir, and Banu Quraizah. It was to these tribes that Muhammad fled after being refused by the Qurayshi of Mecca.[26]

مروج الذهب ج 2ص 152 – المسيحية و الحضارة العربية [26]
ص 82.

Reasons for Conflict between Mecca and Medina

Mecca was known for its trading, business, and high education. Medina was an agricultural society and was also famous for making swords, but they were not an educated people. Because of this, when Mecca started making deals to protect the foreign convoys, they disregarded what Medina had to offer. This offended the people of Medina.

Muhammad's grandfather came from a poor branch of the Quraysh. The rich tribe stole his inheritance, so he left Mecca to live in Medina. It was here that he married a Jewish woman. Then he used his connections with the Jewish in Medina to blackmail the rich Quraysh tribe to give his inheritance back or face the sword. When Muhammad was refused by the Quraysh, he left Mecca to go to his family in Medina.

Muhammad knew that the Jewish people were religious and had a book from God. To influence them to believe in Islam, he told them that they were a blessed people and revealed only good verses from the Quran to them. Then, when he tried to get them to believe that he was a prophet of God, the Jewish people rejected him because all prophets must be Jewish. This made Muhammad angry, so he then claimed that Allah gave him new verses in the Quran to kill the Jews. This is why there are contradictions in the Quran. The first part of the Quran demonstrates love for the Jews, but then later commands their murder. Muhammad fabricated a story that a Jewish man tried

to kill him, so it justified his reasoning for killing the Jewish men, taking their women as slaves, and burning their properties.[27]

THE SCIENCES IN WHICH THE ARABS EXCELLED

Ancient Arabs excelled in many different sciences. Greek science, mainly in Alexandria and Athens, moved to and flourished in the east region (Hijaz and Mecca) Edessa (city in Upper Mesopotamia), Nusaybin (city in Mardin Province, Turkey), Gundeshapur (intellectual center of the Sassanid Empire in Iran), and al-Madaan in the north, south, east, and west.

Schools (*aeskul* in Syrian and *scholae* in Greek) were built next to monasteries. Arabs associated the word *school* with a Christian school or a school that was attached to a monastery. They taught theology, grammar, philosophy, medicine, music, mathematics, and astronomy. Severus Sobokhyt, a Syrian scholar and resident of Kennesrin Monastery (in upper Euphrates), wrote a major treatise on syllogisms (logistical argument that applies to deductive reasoning to arrive at a conclusion based on two or more propositions asserted or assumed to be true). He was also the first person to introduce the Indian number system to other countries.[28]

---

[27] (السيرة النبوية لإبن هشام ، السيرة الحلبية)

[28] قصة الحضارة عصر الإيمان . ص180

In the fifth century, Hepa (Syrian translator) and his student Proba (or Brobos) were followers of the Persian school in Edessa. Hepa translated many books about medicine, astronomy, and poetry into Arabic.[29]

The Muslims say that before Islam, Syria, Iraq, Yemen, and Egypt lived in stupidity without the enlightenment of science. They say that Islam brought knowledge and light to their culture. In reality, these countries already excelled in medicine, poetry, mathematics and science.

Medicine

Arabs excelled in breeding and in detecting and treating diseases in horses, mules, donkeys, and camels.[30]

The most famous book written about horses was found in Ahmediya, a school in Baghdad, and was written by Aby Abdullah Muhammad al-Eskafy. Many veterinarians, like al-Hareth bin Kelda al-Thaqafy retired and moved to Egypt. Thaqafy was a Nestorian from Taif and was educated in Persia and Yemen during the time of Muhammad. He was called "the doctor of Arabs" because he had an important book in medicine called *Almohawara,* which used important phrases like, "the stomach is the home of disease."[31]

المسيحية و الحضارة العربية . جورج شحاته ص 121 - 122 [29]

الألوسي . بلوغ الأرب في معرفة أحوال العرب . ج 3 ص [30] من327 ـ339.

المسيحية و الحضارة العربية ص158 [31]

Ibn Hozayem, one of the most famous doctors, was also a poet. Ibn Alathir said about Hozayem that he was more clever than Thaqafy. Ancient Arabs such as these men were able to diagnose fever, jaundice, headache, flu, cough, urinary retention, gallstone, leprosy, elephantiasis, and a liver disease called *rain*.[32]

Poetry

Arabs were famous for their poetry. They knew their heritage and their lineage through what their grandparents had written to them. Muhammad himself said, "Poetry is wisdom." Omar ibn al-Khattab said, "It is the best thing I have ever learned and I can use it to achieve my goals."

If an ancient Arab tribe had a talented poet, it was customary for all other tribes to come and celebrate by sharing food and music (women played the drums), as was the custom also in wedding banquets. There were many famous poets from this time. Oday ibn Zaid (who died before 590 BC) was a Christian poet who described the creation from the Old Testament in his poems.[33]

Astronomy

Arabs were interested in astronomy—the outer world, strange bodies, and the movement of the planets. Authors such as Aby Qayd, ibn Omar, al-Nahwi, Aby Bakr Muhammad, and Aby al-Hassan al-Nadar wrote books

---

المرجع نفسه ج 3 من ص327 إلى339 [32]

بلوغ الإرب في معرفة أحوال العرب . الآلوسي ج 3 ص82 [33]

about astronomy and the universe. Aby Hanifa al-Demory wrote about times, seasons, wind, the description of the sky, the names for the stars, and the cycle of the moon (zodiac). Some wrote about rain, wind, timing, types of clouds, thunder and lightning, and the science of navigation, the science of lineages, and history.

In the year 773 AD, India had a great impact in this field. Caliph al-Mansour translated *Aserhunta,* which was an Indian message dating back to 425 BC. This helped bring the Indian number system to the Islamic land.[34]

How is it possible that these men wrote about such advanced subjects as astronomy when, as the Muslims claim, they could not read or write?

Divination

Divination is the science of tracking footprints. Arabs distinguished between footprints of men, women and girls, and old and young men to locate fugitives and drifters and follow their tracks, specifically those that were hidden. They were able to recognize these hidden places through the senses and knew the kind of dust and stones that were in every location in the desert, and they used this ability to guide convoys and armies. This science was never used to mislead or disorient anyone for the purpose of perishing.[35]

---

[34] الألوسي . بلوغ الأرب في معرفة أحوال العرب . ج 3 ص223
قصة الحضارة عصر الإيمان . ص180

[35] الألوسي . بلوغ الأرب في معرفة أحوال العرب . ج 3 ص261

Rifle Science (Riyafah)

Riyafah is the science of finding water in the ground. This is done by putting one's ear to the ground or tracking the movement of birds and smelling the dust.[36]

Calligraphy

Arabs were famous for several types of writing called *calligraphy*—including Kafi and Hemyary—which were of extremely high perfection, precision, and quality.[37]

Lineage and Genealogy

Ancient Arabs were very proud of their lineage and would boast about their ancestors. Some of the most famous were Daghfal bin Hanzla, Warqaa al-Ashaar, Zaid ibn Alqyes, and al-Nakhar bin Aws.[38]

During the ancient times, historians recorded the history of many old nations, kings, morals, cultures, and policies, being very careful about how they portrayed the genealogies of the ancients.

The Arab people were so proud of their heritage that anyone who questioned (without the witness of four people) the genealogy of a particular person was to be whipped with eighty lashes.[39] Lineage was so

---

[36] الألوسي . بلوغ الأرب في معرفة أحوال العرب . ج 3 ص343

[37] الألوسي . بلوغ الأرب في معرفة أحوال العرب . ج 3 ص344

[38] الألوسي . بلوغ الأرب في معرفة أحوال العرب . ج 3 ص102,181

[39] الإسلام بين الدولة الدينية و المدنية ص 153

important for the Arab people that they had historians who specialized in the study of ancestry.

Because the culture or civilization of Islam was born from the land and did not come down from heaven, the Quran once again adopted the practice of the Arab people:

> *As for those who accuse chaste women and do not bring four witnesses, strike them eighty lashes, and never accept any testimony from them after that, and they are transgressors.*[40]

Arab Architecture

Architecture styles in ancient times were taken from the Levant. Mosques were built like a minaret (from the Babylonian edifice), while the bell tower represented the Christian churches. Indian Muslims shaped their mosques in the form of the country, like a cylinder. African Muslims were influenced by Alexandria, using the four corners.[41]

SUMMARY

Through this chapter, you have seen the great logic, economy, business, and culture that the Arab people had established before the introduction of Islam. Because they were rich and educated, the religion

---

[40] Sura 24:4

تاريخ العرب في عصر الجاهلية . ص420 [41]

Muhammad offered was weak. In fact, after ten years of preaching Islam in Mecca, he only had 72 converts, most of whom were among his relatives and friends. He then resorted to the sword to propagate Islam. When he came by the sword, all people either converted to Islam or were killed.

4

ARAB LEADERSHIP BEFORE MUHAMMAD

The existence of a Holy Book in Christianity and Judaism influenced the religious foundation of the Arab tribes significantly, playing an important role in the mindset of the Arabs. The Jews believed in a Messiah as a King who would come one day, fight, claim victory, and rule over all nations. This doctrine of a coming Jewish Messiah intrigued the Arab tribes.

The Arab tribes lived independently of each other and were even hostile toward each other. Each tribe had their own idols, although they did not worship their idols.

Some wise thinkers of the day realized that they needed a religion to unify them, a religion that would transcend morality, offering more than simply laws against violence and murder. Muhammad was one of

these thinkers, and he took the ideas and cultures of these tribes to make his prophecies.

While you are reading this chapter, ask these questions:

- *If the Arab community was teaching the same principles and ideas of the Quran, should not each of these men also be accepted as a prophet from god?*

- *If Muhammad's message was different than that of the Arab tribes and was really from god, why then did he reject them and yet adapt their teaching?*

Zaid ibn Amr, Quss ibn Saidah, Khalid ibn Sinan, Umayyah ibn Abi as-Salt, Abd al-Muttalib, and Waraqa ibn Nawfal influenced many of the Arabs with their religious views. Let's take a look at who these people were and what is written in history about them to help explain.

Zaid ibn Amr

The history books mention that Zaid ibn Amr became a Jew, then turned to Christianity, and then became a follower of the Al-Ahnaf religion (a religion of Abraham). He did not worship idols or offer sacrifices to them; he didn't eat animals found dead or anything with blood in it; and he refused usury. He also followed the religion of Abraham and died before Muhammad's prophecy was given. Zaid taught the idea of oneness.

One of his arguments went something like this:

Do you believe in one god or in many gods?

Do you believe in one religion or in many religions?

If you had to swear by one god and one religion, which one would you choose?

He taught his people that if they feared god and respected him, then at the end of their life, they would be in his paradise.

Zaid taught about respect for parents, respect for all prophets and their messages, and that anyone who did good deeds would be in paradise and those who were bad would be in hell. He also taught that god held up the sky without pillars for support.

Muhammad used these same teachings in the beginning of Islam. When Muhammad was initially trying to convince his Qurayshi tribe that he was a prophet from god, he taught that Zaid would be in paradise with himself and Christ. Later, when he gained power through bloodshed, he called Zaid an infidel.[42]

---

42 السيرة النبوية لإبن هشام . ج ١   ص١٤٢

، أسد الغابة في معرفة أحوال الصحابة . للأثير. ج2 ص269

محمد . كارين أرمسترونج ص110

بلوغ الأرب ج2 من ص247 حتى 251

Quss ibn Saidah

Quss ibn Saidah was one of the wisest Arabs and a famous philosopher, and he was well loved by the people. He was the first of the Arabs to believe in resurrection after death. He was the first to hold a staff in his hand while preaching. Quss taught that the sky was a ceiling to the earth. Muhammad copied this idea into the Quran in Sura 21:32. Quss ibn Saidah also died before Muhammad's prophecy was given.

Although considered an infidel when he died, Muhammad said that he was about to become a Muslim. Muhammad often asked his friends to recite Quss' teachings. If Quss was considered an infidel, then why would Muhammad want to hear his teachings?[43]

Khalid ibn Sinan

Khalid ibn Sinan also followed the Al-Ahnaf religion and the doctrine of oneness. The Arab tribes accepted him as a prophet.

Muhammad taught that Khalid ibn Sinan was a prophet but lost his way because of his tribe. When Khalid was dying, he asked his people to bury him and guard his grave. He told them that if they saw and heard a tailless donkey walking and braying near his cemetery plot, they were to dig him up and he would tell them what he had seen and what he wanted. But they did not do what he asked because they were afraid to be accused of unearthing graves.[44]

In one of the well-known stories about Khalid, his people were complaining to him that phoenix birds were attacking and eating their children and animals. Khalid prayed and god caused these birds to become extinct.[45]

Another story was told about a fire that split a mountain. When the people saw this, they were afraid and thought it was god. They were going to begin worshipping the fire as the Magi do. However, Khalid then entered the fire and extinguished it.[46]

Later, when Muhammad was teaching, he said these words:

Say, "He is Allah, the one and only. Allah the eternal, absolute. He begetteth not, nor is he begotten. And there is none like unto him."[47]

Khalid's daughter heard him speak these words and said, "I heard my father saying the same words."[48]

The Quran says:

---

[44] مروج الذهب ج ٢ ص٢٢٨

[45] روج الذهب ج ١ ص٧٩ ـ اسد الغابة ج ٢ ص٩٩
بلوغ الإرب ج2ص 279

[46] بلوغ الإرب ج2ص 279

[47] Sura 112:1-4

[48] أسد الغابة ج 2 ص 99 ـ مروج الذهب ج 1 ص 79 ـ بلوغ الإرب ج 2ص 279

Nothing keeps us from sending signs except that the former peoples denied them.[49]

It teaches that Muhammad never did any miracles. However, Islamic biographies show that Khalid ibn Sinan performed these miracles. Which of these men was greater?

Umayyah ibn Abi as-Salt

Umayyah ibn Abi as-Salt's original name was Abdullah ibn Rabea bin Auf. He was one of the leaders of the Thaqif tribe, which traded in the Levant. He was a very famous poet who wrote about religious issues that described the land, sun, moon, angels and prophets, resurrection, and heaven and hell. He used unusual expressions specifically for the Arabs. Umayyah was a learned man who read many books.

Umayyah also believed in the doctrine of oneness and did not worship idols. He refused wine and believed in prayer and fasting. He dressed in sackcloth in humility to seek god's favor. He died in 630 AD.[50]

Umayyah said some creatures with wings came from heaven, split his chest, and removed his heart. The creatures cleaned his heart and prepared him for prophecy.[51]

---

[49] Sura 17:59

[50] المسيحية و الحضارة العربية . ص 148 ـ مروج الذهب ج 1 ص 81

[51] الحزب الهاشمي.ص 120 .سيد القمني .

In the Quran, Muhammad claimed that as a child, he played with his milk kinship brother (they were both nursed by the same woman) behind the house of Bani Saad. There was a third child with them. God sent three angels to split Muhammad's chest to prepare him for prophecy, like Umayyah. But when the angels came, they did not recognize Muhammad. So the angels conferred and decided to choose the one who was the most beautiful. They chose Muhammad.[52]

Umayyah described the creatures on Allah's throne as a man, a bull, an eagle, and a lion. He also said that eight creatures carried the throne of God. In the Bible, we read:

...the first living creature like a lion, the second living creature like an ox, the third living creature with the face of a man, and the fourth living creature like an eagle in flight.[53]

And in the Quran:

And the angels will be on its sides, and eight will, that day, bear the throne of thy lord above them.[54]

---

[52] المسيحية و الحضارة العربية ص١٤٨ ـ مروج الدهب و معادن الجوهر ١- ص٨١

[53] Revelation 4:7

[54] Sura 69:17

Umayyah learned from the Bible, and Muhammad learned from Umayyah.[55] Islam's teaching was
very close to that of Umayyah. Muhammad said that
Umayyah was an infidel at heart, but Muhammad
believed in his poetry.

Abd al-Muttalib

Abd al-Muttalib bin Hashim (Muhammad's grandfather) united the hearts of the Arabs under one god,
eliminating statues and idols, mediations and interces-
sors. He was one of the leaders of the Al-Ahnaf religion,
which aimed at unifying politics through the belief in
monotheism.

Muttalib had a vision, so he dug the well at Zamzam
and was the first to provide water for pilgrims. Muttalib created the Kaaba doctrine (the beginning of
circumambulation, or walking around the holy Black
Stone). He recommended that each person take care
of his own relatives and feed the poor. He believed in
resurrection after death. He kept all promises, taught
his followers to love their enemies, and forbade the
drinking of wine. He also commanded that all adulter-
ers were to be stoned.[56]

The tradition in the Arab tribes was that when any
man had ten male children, he would sacrifice the
youngest son to god. Abd al-Muttalib's youngest son,

Abdullah (Muhammad's father) was the one closest to his heart. He did not want to sacrifice his son, so he sought counsel from some wise men in Yemen. They suggested that he cast lots between ten camels and Abdullah. Each time the lot fell on Abdullah, he was to increase the camels by ten until the lot fell on the camels. Then he should give the cost of that number of camels to the poor to redeem his son. He cast lots by shaking two arrows between Abdullah and the ten camels. Muttalib had increased the number of camels to one hundred before the lot fell on the camels. He then redeemed his son for the price of one hundred camels. He fulfilled the vow he made to god, creating some morals that are now in the Quran. It was because of this story that Islamic law now says that when one man kills another, the murderer must pay the cost of one hundred camels to the victim's family.

As a result, the Quraysh said that Muttalib was the second Abraham. He died at the age of one hundred and twenty, when Muhammad was eight years old. Muttalib was the first to be washed with water and perfume upon his death, and was dressed in two suits of Yemen, which were equivalent to one thousand grams of gold.[57]

Most of the morals Muhammad created were taken from his grandfather. Muhammad also said that god rewards the obedient and punishes the disobedient.

تاريخ اليعقوبي . ج ٢ ص١٠ و١١ و١٤ [57]

He taught his followers to fulfill vows and to offer one hundred camels as blood money. He also prohibited the drinking of alcohol, adultery, and marrying one's sister, mother, or aunt.

Waraqa ibn Nawfal

Waraqa ibn Nawfal, the cousin of Khadija (Muhammad's first wife), was from a Christian tribe and read the books of the Jews and Christians. He believed in Moses' religion (Judaism), then Christianity, and kept the Torah and the Gospel. The Quran says:

> *Say, o people of the scripture, you are standing on nothing until you uphold the laws of the Torah and Gospel.*[58]

Many scholars think that Waraqa converted to Christianity as many of the Arab tribes did in his day (though the Christianity of this time was a false Christianity, not holding to all of the truths of the Bible). Historians disagree about whether he died as a Christian or as a believer in Islam. They do agree that he refrained from eating anything found dead or anything with blood in it, and did not offer sacrifices to idols.

Before he died, Waraqa told Khadija that he thought Muhammad was a prophet (the Christian definition of a prophet is one who encourages and exhorts the church). Because Waraqa and Khadija were from a Christian tribe, when Muhammad told them about his

[58] Sura 5:68

dreams and visions, they thought God was calling him to be a missionary to his family. Because of this, Khadija encouraged him to stop working and go to meditate and learn. During the lifetime of Waraqa and Khadija, Muhammad spoke gently and kindly about Christians and Jews. He was also the husband of one wife only while married to Khadija. But after Waraqa died, Muhammad's dreams and visions ceased. The Quraysh tribes said that after Waraqa was dead, Muhammad's inspiration was dead also.[59]

SUMMARY

Each of these people influenced Muhammad's thinking and heart. He adopted their ideas, principles, and teachings about Islam, using the same words, descriptions, and terminologies.

Here are some questions for you to consider:

- *Why didn't those who lived in the same time with Muhammad convert to Islam?*

- *Why were all these people not considered a reference for Islam rather than infidels of Islam?*

- *These people read books, saw visions, and performed miracles, but Muhammad*

---

[59] تفسير سورة اقرأ . إبن كثير ، الكامل في التاريخ . إبن الأثير ج 1 ص577

never did any of these things. Why then did Muhammad call these people infidels?

- *Muslims believe that Muhammad was illiterate—able to neither read nor write. The Quran confirms that Muhammad did not perform any miracles. Muhammad adopted all of his rules, ideas, and faith from these men. Why then should he be believed?*

PART II

5

Religious
Background

There is much evidence to prove that many different religions, including monotheism (Nasraniah and Judaism), heathenism, worship of idols, and worship of the sun and moon, all existed inside the Arabian Peninsula before Islam. Evidence also disproves false claims that Arabs did not know god. Arabs were divided as a result of these different belief systems, which influenced their society's economy and politics. These differences also dangerously impacted Arabs' thinking, causing them to accept Islam.

Even though Mecca was considered the city of infidels, the people had the freedom to declare their belief in whatever they wanted to. After Islam, the Arabs lost this freedom. When Islam came, the freedom to believe in any other religion was denied—no religion would be accepted other than Islam. Those who had

emigrated from Mecca to Yathrib and converted to Islam were considered to be better than native Yathrib people. A strong believer was better than a weak one; a warrior was better than one who had not fought.

JUDAISM AND THE JEWISH PEOPLE

Jews settled in the Arabian Peninsula several centuries before Islam. They vehemently resisted and denied Muhammad's message. The Quran says:

> *O Children of Israel! Remember my favor that I have bestowed upon you and that I preferred you over the worlds.[60]*

Immigration of the Jews to the Arabian Peninsula

Jews were persecuted by the Romans in Jerusalem and were scattered. After the destruction of the temple in Jerusalem in 70 AD, groups of Jews moved to the Arabian Peninsula, settling in places like Hijaz, Yathrib, Fedek, Khaybar, Temaa, and Yemen.

Some of the famous Jewish settlements in the Arabian Peninsula were Yemen and Hijaz. Jews who had settled in Yemen spread Judaism across the south, converting some of the people to Judaism.[61]

---

[60] Sura 2:47, Sura 2:122

[61] تاريخ العرب في عصر الجاهلية ص 392
د /جواد على المفصل في تاريخ العرب قبل الإسلام ص 519

The Most Famous Jews in the Arabian Peninsula

Zu Nwas was one of the most famous Yemeni who turned to Judaism. He was known for his enthusiasm of Judaism and persecution of the Christians in Najran.

The most well known Jewish tribes—Banu Quraizah, Banu Nadir, and Banu Qaynuqa—lived in Yathrib. Other tribes, such as Banu Aws and Banu Zaura, spread Judaism, impacting the pagan Arab tribes.[62]

The Laws and Teachings of Judaism

The Jews presented things like the Ten Commandments:

"You shall have no other gods before Me. You shall not make for yourself a carved image (idol), or any likeness of anything that is in heaven above, or that is on the earth beneath, or that is in the water under the earth..."[63]

They also followed the doctrine of monotheism:

"Hear, O Israel: The LORD our God, the LORD is one."[64]

Even the law of war according to Deuteronomy 20:1-14 proves Jewish legislation existed in the Arabian Peninsula centuries before Islam.

---

[62] فجر الإسلام . أحمد أمين ص 41

[63] Deuteronomy 5:7-21

[64] Deuteronomy 6:4

The belief in the existence of one God and the rejection of the belief in multiple gods and idolatry was spread among a large number of Arab tribes in the Arabian Peninsula during this time. Al-Ahnaf was affected more than the others in its acceptance of this belief.

Jewish Influence Over the Arab Tribes

A rumor began spreading among the Arabs claiming a prophet would soon come to set the people free from their suffering and persecution, bringing peace to his followers. This is the doctrine of the Jewish Messiah.[65]

Arabs began using new terminology, like *faith, reward, resurrection, hell,* and *devil.* Umayyah ibn Abi as-Salt's poetry included an abundance of Jewish theology, teaching, and expressions. Also, Waraqa ibn Nawfal read, wrote, and spoke Hebrew. Waraqa was the first to translate the Old Testament into Arabic.

Fifteen years after Muhammad married Khadija, he declared his prophecy. Nothing is written in Muhammad's biography to describe this era. Muslim scholars hide anything that proves Muhammad was not a prophet and that the Quran is not from Allah. Therefore, there are many pieces of history missing.

It is well known that Jewish law is not limited to worship or morality; rather, it deals with life in all dimensions (like punishing people for crimes committed). These laws seriously affected Muhammad's ability to create a Qurayshi state in Yathrib, because they gave him rules and boundaries that made Islam impossible for him to establish.

Just as Moses led the people in the name of God, Muhammad endeavored to lead the people in the name of Allah.[66]

NASRANIAH (FALSE CHRISTIANITY)

Nasraniah (from Aramaic "Nazarene," not referring to the modern day Nazarene church) is not true Christianity; it is a false denomination that came out of Nazareth. The Quran refers to all people who believe in Jesus as Nazarenes, or Nasraniah. It does not call them Christians, because Muhammad believed that Nasraniah was true Christianity.

The Nasraniah were divided into several factions, including Alabuniah, Nestorianism, Marianism, and Arianism. In the Quran, Muhammad says:

Then the factions differed [concerning Jesus] from among them, so woe to those who disbelieved from the scene of tremendous day.[67]

Before Islam, the Arabian Peninsula was surrounded by Christian nations, such as Syria (from the north), Iraq (from the northeast), Yemen (from the south), and

---

فجر الإسلام . أحمد أمين ص 41 [66]

[67] Sura 19:37

Ethiopia (from the west). Christianity spread inside
the Arabian Peninsula across geographic, political,
and economic borders. Christian tribes within these
nations—Tanokh, Hemyar, Taghleb, Ghassan, Kodaa,
Lakhmen, Taai, and Tamim—surrounded the Peninsula
from all directions.[68]

The Political Background of Nasraniah In the Arabian Peninsula

Politically, Christians (most from al-Yaakeba (Jacobins)) sought refuge and freedom from the severe
persecution of the Romans during the second century after Christ was born. Christianity spread among
Yemeni tribes, such as Taghleb, Ghassan, and Kodaa,
after Ethiopia invaded the northern and southern
parts of Yemen.

The people living in Najran, the most famous Christian city in the south of the Peninsula, accepted the
doctrine of the Jacobins. They had more contact with
the Ethiopians than with the Romans, allowing Nasraniah to last until the era of Omar. Most of them eventually evacuated to Iraq (the Levant).

Later on, it was thought that the Romans extended
their influence in the region by spreading Christianity
at the hands of clerics who preached it.[69]

المسيحية و الحضارة العربية . جورج. ص 145 [68]

فـجر الإسلام . أحمد أمين . ص 44, 45 [69]

The Economy of Nasraniah

Economically, the Arabs of the Peninsula—in particular those who lived in the north—were in contact with Ghassanids and al-Manazera Christians. Convoys of believers from Syria were arriving in the Arabian Peninsula (Hijaz) between the two rivers.

The region was full of churches and monasteries, where travelers would stay the night. The people on these convoys would hear many of the Nasraniah stories and themes. Unfortunately, the stories told were not those of true Christianity.[70]

Some of these tribes sold leather and silk. There was also mutual cooperation between the nobles of al-Hirah (small Nasraniah kingdom in Iraq) and those of the Quraysh.[71]

Nasraniah and Jewish tribes were rich and famous, with a strong economy. Muhammad became covetous of their wealth; this also helped to spur his decision to destroy and plunder them in the name of Islam.

In biblical times, Arabs were in Jerusalem on the Day of Pentecost.[72] So, it is probable that at least some of these Arabs were either Jews or Christians and that they feared and worshipped God. When the Apostle Paul went to Damascus after his conversion, the city

---

تاريخ العرب في العصر الجاهلي ص٣١١ ، ٤٨٥ [70]

الإسلام من القبلية للدولة المركزية . ص170 [71]

[72] Acts 2:11

was in the hands of King al-Harith, a Ghassanid king.[73] He had ruled from 9 BC to 40 AD, which means Arabs had received the message of true Christianity.[74]

FAMOUS NASRANIAH TRIBES

The most famous Nasraniah tribes in the Arabian Peninsula at that time were Ghassanids and Lakhmen.

Ghassanids

Originally from the Jaffina tribe, the Ghassanids were from Syria and had emigrated from Yemen. They had been connected to the Roman Empire since the fourth century, and were a shield against the negativity of the Arab tribes and Persians. It had been known that the kings of Ghassan built several monasteries, such as the Hend Monastery of Haly and the Ayoub Monastery. These two monasteries helped to evangelize and convert Arabs to the Nasraniah faith.[75]

Lakhmen

Romans and Persians had agents on the borders. Lakhmen settled in the capital, al-Hirah, and Arabs secured the Persian borders. This closeness to the Persians allowed them to be more urbanized and

---

[73] 2 Corinthians 11:32

[74] المسيحية و الحضارة العربية .الأب /جورج شحاته. ص 57 و58

[75] المسيحية و الحضارة العربية ص67 محمد . كارين أرمسترونج ص 87

better thinkers than the Arabs of the Peninsula. Some of them were introduced to Christianity by missionaries, while others joined the Hend Monastery after Alnoman the Fifth built it.

The commercialism in al-Hirah helped spread this tribe's beliefs in nature among the Arabs. The writer of the Book of Songs mentioned that Alasha, the poet, spread his religious views of Christianity as he traveled across the Arabian Peninsula.[76]

NASRANIAH IN MECCA

The people of Mecca were able to see the evidence in favor of monotheism in drawings of prophets and angels on the walls of the Kaaba. These beings were mentioned in Bible stories, along with stories of Jesus and His mother Mary.

Al-Azroki (writer of Muhammad's biography) narrated a story that says:

On the day of opening Mecca, the prophet Muhammad requested a piece of cloth wet with water from the well of Zamzam and started to remove all photos from the walls of the Kaaba, except the photo of Jesus and His mother. Muhammad looked at the photo of Abraham and he said, "Kill the Nasraniah who

المسيحية و الحضارة العربية ص 76 ، محمد. كارين أرمسترونج ص 88 [76]

*live in Mecca because they teach that Abra-
ham was sick."*[77]

The Nasraniah in Mecca were brought from Ethiopia to work as slaves for the masters of the Quraysh.
There were also some Nasraniah from Rome, like
Suhayb ar-Rumi, a slave for wealthy people, like Abdullah ibn Judan.[78] The Quran says:

> *Surely we know well that they say about you:
> "It is only a human being who teaches him,"
> (notwithstanding) that he whom they mali-
> ciously hint at is of foreign tongue, while this
> (Quran) is plain Arabic speech.*[79]

Al-Qurtubi, one of the great scholars of Islam,
explained this verse: "The Quraysh many times saw
Muhammad sitting with ar-Rumi talking together. The
Quraysh told Muhammad, 'ar-Rumi is teaching you
about the Bible.' Muhammad said, 'No, I talk to him
about Islam.'"

Qurtubi continued to say that the problem is that
ar-Rumi did not speak Arabic; he spoke Greek. The
problem is that Muslims believe Muhammad was illiterate and did not know how to read, write, or speak any
other language but Arabic. So if ar-Rumi spoke Greek
and Muhammad spoke Arabic, how did they commu-

المسيحية و الحضارة العربية. الأب د /جورج شحاته ص 83 [77]

البداية و النهاية.ج 3 ص 173 [78]

[79] Sura 16:103

nicate together? Or did Muhammad also speak Greek?
This is the most logical conclusion for their communi-
cation, and when they argued, it is quite probable that
Muhammad learned much about Nasraniah.[80]

EGYPTIAN COPTIC IN MECCA

The Copts in Egypt formed a Christian denomination similar to the Catholic denomination. Some of
the Egyptian Coptic and Ethiopian slaves in Mecca
participated in building the Kaaba. When the Kaaba
was submerged by a flood, these slaves brought wood
from the wreckage of a ship that had sunk in the
Shuaiba Port near Jeddah, a small city on the Red Sea
near Saudi Arabia. This fact is confirmed by al-Kandy,
an Islamic historian, and took place 743 years before
Jesus walked the earth.[81]

INSIGHTS ABOUT CHRISTIANITY IN THE QURAN

When we talk about the tribes that converted to
Christianity, we must pay attention to what the Quran
says about Nasraniah, because most of these tribes
were not true Christians. They believed in Christian

---

[80] Sura 16:103 أسباب النزول ـ 117ص 10تفسي تفسير القرطبي ج
للسيوطي سبب نزول سورة النحل آية16

[81] هوامش الفتح العربي لمصر. ص10
قصة الحضارة عبر الايمان ص١١
الكندي فضائل مصر ص٢٨ . هوامش الفتح العربي ص١٠

heresies that advocated against the teachings of the Church and the Bible.

The Quran does not say anything about the early fundamental characteristics or principles of the early Christians, like Saul (later named Paul), who had the greatest impact in missionary history in spreading the Gospel.

The Quran does not say anything about the Council of Nicaea in 325 AD (the first ecumenical council of the Christian Church); the persecution of the disciples for spreading their message; or the four Gospels (Matthew, Mark, Luke, and John), even though they were available to Christians from centuries earlier, who claimed that God himself inspired and appointed men to write these Gospels.

The reader of the Quran senses a massive difference between talking about Jews and handling Christianity. In her book, *Muhammad: A Biography of the Prophet*, Karen Armstrong comments about how, at the beginning of the seventh century, the impression of true Christianity was distorted among the Arabs of the Arabian Peninsula, especially in the surrounding states where people believed in these misrepresentations. While the Bedouins were impressed with the Nasraniah church in Najran, they were still suspicious of their religious systems.[82]

---

[82] Karen Armstrong, *Muhammad: A Biography of the Prophet*, 88.
ص٨٨ النبي محمد . كارين أرمسترونج

We can imagine the number of misguided teachings considered to be true Christianity that reached the Arabian Peninsula, and how far Islam was from the truth. Because of the presence of Coptic Egyptians, Nasraniah Ethiopians, and Jews in Mecca, the Arab tribes were familiar with the teachings of Nasraniah and Judaism. For this reason, great Arab leaders took much of their teachings from the influence of Christianity, Nasraniah, and Judaism. The Arab tribes had culture, civilization, and concepts of god, even though some of their views were distorted. Islam tried to hide and even erase the reality that these three religions had an effect on the culture, education, ethics, and practices of the Arabian Peninsula.

Let's look at these heretical teachings that were spread in closed countries.

EBIONITES

Ebionites (meaning *poor ones* in Hebrew) were a sect of Judeo-Christians from Nazareth, the hometown of Jesus Christ, with a belief in monotheism (Nasraniah). Their doctrine was a mixture of Judaism and Christianity, with belief in God the Creator.

They believed that Jesus was a prophet, but denied His divinity—that He is the Son of God. Saturdays were set aside as holy days. They did not believe that Jesus was crucified, but rather that it was someone else like Him. This is the sect that Saul had persecuted. They

later escaped to places like Mecca, Najran, and the valley of villages (the middle and west of the Peninsula). In defiance, they stopped mentioning the name of Saul—their persecutor and enemy—and described his followers as infidels.

They believed in only one Gospel, while they believed the other Gospels were corrupted. They believed that God created Jesus in Mary's womb.[83]

GNOSTICISM

Gnosticism is a Greek word meaning knowledge or signs of spiritual and divine matters. It is a mixture of philosophies and beliefs in Christianity, Judaism, Platonism, and Persian influences.

They believed in two gods—a god of goodness and a god of evil. They believed that material is evil and that the god of goodness is far from that evil substance. They believed that Christ did not take the body of a human. They believed that the Virgin Mary remained a virgin even after the birth of Christ—that the passage of Jesus through her womb was like the passage of light through glass.[84]

دائرة المعارف الكتابية للكتاب المقدس ج 1ص 55 [83]
تاريخ الفكر المسيحي . عوض سمعان

تاريخ الفكر المسيحي . القس . حنا الخضري ـ دائرة المعرف الكتابية [84]
للكتاب المقدس

NESTORIANISM

Nestorius was a monk from Antioch and became the Patriarch of Constantinople in 428 AD. The doctrine of *Nestorianism* emphasizes that Jesus Christ had two distinct natures or persons—one human and one divine. Nestorians believed these two natures were distinct from each other before birth.

They believed that the Jesus who was born, felt pain, grew tired, and died was the human Jesus; while the Jesus who performed miracles and rose from the grave was the divine Jesus. Anything that was supernatural was considered to be from the divine Jesus. Thus, they believe in a worn nature and a dressed-up nature.

Nestorius and his followers were expelled from the Church as heretics after the Council of Ephesus was created in 431 AD.[85]

ARIANISM

Arius was Libyan. Nothing is known about his family—whether they were Christian or pagan—only that he was born in Kairouan in 270 AD. It is believed that he studied theology in Antioch (although some say that he studied theology in Alexandria). He lived in Egypt and tried to spread his deviant teachings among the church there. Arius was directly influenced by

---

تاريخ الكنيسة القبطية ـ تاريخ الفكر المسيحي ـ المسيحية و الحضارة [85]
العربية

a teacher named Lukianos (Saint Lucian), who some believe to be his godfather.

Arius taught that God is one God and that He is eternal, not born of flesh. He believed the Son existed before the creation of the world, but He is not eternal; He was born like all other creations, according to the will of God. He taught that the Christ whom Christians worship is not God and does not have divine attributes, such as omniscience, omnipotence, etc. He believed that Christ's knowledge is limited, not absolute; therefore, He cannot represent the Father completely. He believed the Father created the Son (the Word) for us and so is a creature like us—changeable. He was free to remain good as the Father created Him, or to fall away and become evil, as Satan did.[86]

Monasteries and missionary movements related to the Arian doctrine were spread throughout the Arabian Peninsula. After the persecution they faced from the Tatars and Turks, they went to India, China, and Tibet. Now, there are some Arian churches in Iraq, Syria, and the United States.

MARIANISM

A Marist was a member of the Roman Catholic Society of Mary, devoted to education at the beginning of 400 AD. The followers of this doctrine believed in the divinity of the Virgin Mary instead of the gods they had worshiped before—including Venus, the Queen of Heaven. Mary was worshiped in the east and west, alongside Venus of the Romans, Aphrodite of Greece, Ishtar of Babylonia, and Ashtoreth of Phoenicia.

The ancient Jews took on these forms of worship, and God severely punished them.[87] They began calling themselves Marists, relating to the unleavened bread that they presented in the Virgin's name.

In ancient times, pagans believed that their gods could marry their women and have children. In this way, Marists believed that a god married the Virgin Mary and she gave birth to the Lord Jesus Christ. By the end of the seventh century, the church resisted the doctrine of the Marists.[88]

Muhammad fought the people in these Christian communities and wanted "the infidels driven out from the Arabian Peninsula." He thought these religions were true Christianity.[89]

HOW NASRANIAH (FALSE CHRISTIANITY) AND JUDAISM NURTURED ISLAM

Nasraniah left a profound impact on the Arabs in the Arabian Peninsula, especially in ideology. The priests and monks preached in the market places,

---

[87] Jeremiah 7:18-20, 44:19

تاريخ الفكر المسيحي . دائرة المعارف الكتابية للكتاب المقدس [88]

الطبقات الكبرى لأبن سعد ج2 ص242 ، الدفاع عن محمد ضد [89]
المنتقصين من قدره . ص138

teaching the people about resurrection, paradise, fire, and other concepts taught in the Quran. Much of the Quran reports their view and expressions and through this, the doctrine of monotheism was birthed as the correct and true doctrine.

Before Nasraniah, Judaism laid the foundation for monotheism, or the worship of one God. Judaism taught the concepts of many ideas, which were later added to the Quran as inspiration from Allah, such as:

- God created the sky without pillars;

- the Earth was flat with an edge; and

- Abraham was willing to sacrifice his son Isaac.[90]

The doctrine of monotheism, which the two religions spread among the Arabs, helped dismantle the basis of idolatry and polytheism and exposed its falsity. Nasraniah and Judaism were key in shaping the views of the Arabs, motivating them to be unified in their religion. The Jewish tribes of Alos and Khazraj (the two largest tribes in Yathrib) welcomed Muhammad into their midst, and it was here that he adopted their religion of monotheism.

The doctrine of monotheism unified power and heavenly authority into one denomination. Before this time, there was freedom of religion and each tribe had its own idol, leader, and priest. Monotheism formed a state where unification called for one god and one ruler to govern them.

It was the same in the days of Moses, when he led the Jews out of Israel and was set up as their leader and advocate between God and man. God gave authority to Moses to lead the people in His name and gave him the Ten Commandments by which to govern His chosen people. Anyone who refused the leadership of Moses was disciplined by God. Following Moses' example, Muhammad set himself up as an authority from Allah, and took the reins of the theocratic religion. However, instead of a religion based on relationship and covenants, he used the religion to colonize, rule, or destroy all tribes and nations. Muhammad became a dictator and used his authority to kill and destroy any who did not follow his teachings from Allah.

Muhammad claimed that Allah gave him authorization to set up a political and religious culture to govern all people, thereby eradicating the freedom of religion and democracy in politics. He set up laws that contributed to the idea of a person taking responsibility for his own actions. Through reward and punishment, not only in the afterlife, but also in this world, Muhammad gave power to punish any violators of crimes such as murder, adultery, and drunkenness. The use of this doctrine and these principles were the pillars and foundation for the success of the Quraysh state.[91]

الإسلام من القبلية للدولة المركزية ص185 [91]

Arab tribes often gave their sons names like Adam, Abraham, and Isaac. This further shows the effect of Nasraniah and Judaism on Islam and demonstrates how familiar the teachings of the Old Testament were among the Arab tribes and how they respected the prophets of God. Muhammad's friends were Adam bin Rabia, Ibrahim bin Harith, Isaac al-Ghannawi, and Abu Ayyub al-Ansari (Ayyub means Job). In fact, Ayyub was Muhammad's host in Yathrib. The Arabs gave their daughters names like Mary, Miriam, Eve, and Hannah. Muhammad also had friends with these names.[92]

AL-AHNAF AND MONOTHEISM

Arab history does not have much written about the Al-Ahnaf religion. The religion itself is mystical and foggy. This religion took much from Judaism and Nasraniah and was known as the religion of Abraham.

A group of wise Arabs followed the practices of monotheism and the religion of Abraham, kept themselves from idol worship, and did not convert to Judaism or Nasraniah. They knew that having faith in one god was wiser than worshiping idols. Some of the leaders from this religion were Waraqa ibn Nawfal, Quss ibn Saidah, Umayyah ibn Abi as-Salt, Abd al-Muttalib, and Zaid ibn Amr.[93]

أسد الغابة في معرفة أحوال الصحابة . باب النسا [92]

قصة الحضارة عصر الإيمان ص24ـ دراسات في تاريخ العرب ، [93]
العرب قبل الإسلام ص 438

It was well known that Zaid was from Al-Ahnaf before Islam—he did not offer sacrifices to idols, get drunk, or eat pork. In fact, he was homeless, lived in the wilderness with the beasts of the desert, and read books.[94]

Zaid ibn Amr and Umayyah ibn Abi as-Salt isolated themselves in caves for meditation and worship. They called for the prohibition of alcohol, eating pork, and eating anything found dead or with blood. They proclaimed a Day of Judgment, rewards for good deeds, and punishment for bad deeds. They banned incest and naked circumambulation around the Kaaba, and insisted on feeding the poor. They encouraged a pilgrimage to the Kaaba, the stoning of Satan, and the sacrifice of sheep, cows, or camels.[95]

Abd al-Muttalib (Muhammad's grandfather) was the guardian of Muhammad and taught him the ways of Al-Ahnaf. When Muhammad claimed that he was a prophet from Allah, he copied all the rules from Al-Ahnaf regarding the pilgrimage to the Kaaba and said that these were new rules from Allah. Al-Ahnaf prepared the way for Islam by its teachings and rules.[96]

WORSHIP OF IDOLS

Idolaters believed in a creator, but denied the existence of the apostles. They did not believe in the

---

فجر الإسلام . أحمد أمين ص 46 [94]

بلوغ الأرب في معرفة أحوال العرب ج2 ص197 [95]

تاريخ العرب في عصر الجاهلية ص490 [96]

resurrection, but believed in reincarnation. They worshiped idols for several reasons, including using them to get closer to god. After a leader died, the people would create a monument of him and worship the image in hopes that their leader would make intercession for them to god.

Amr bin Rabea set up idols and worshiped them after he became ill and moved to the Levant to recover by taking a bath in the well of hot water. He saw the people of the Levant worshiping idols and took some of them with him to Mecca and installed them around the Kaaba.[97]

To be close to Allah, the Quran mentions the worship of Lat and Uzza, idols in the Kaaba:

Have you considered Lat and Uzza?[98]

Ibn Kathir (a highly influential Sunni scholar) said that these idols were in the image of angels or the daughters of god, and could intercede on behalf of the people. The Quran says:

We only worship them so that they may bring us near to Allah.[99]

---

[97] بلوغ الأرب ج2 ص 201

[98] Sura 53:19

[99] Sura 39:3
أبن كثير ـ سورة الزمر ـ أية3 ج4 ، بلوغ الأرب ج2 ص205
تاريخ العرب في عصر الجاهلية ص473

As mentioned earlier, each tribe had their own idol that would bring the people close to Allah. They also set up these idols so that the people would know which direction to best be heard by Allah. Muhammad used the Kaaba as the direction for prayer, because this is what Al-Ahnaf taught him. This is why Muslims pray facing the Kaaba in Mecca in the east.[100]

ZOROASTRIANISM

Zoroastrianism (Zaradasht) was practiced inside Persia and called for the worship of one god—Ahura Mazda, the god of the light and the sky. It was told that at his birth, a loud guffaw was heard and all the evil spirits and demons were scattered and beaten. The idea of goodness and evil was Zaradasht's main focus—he kept people away who practiced strict self-denial as a measure of personal or spiritual discipline (asceticism).

While Zaradasht was standing on top of a mountain and thinking, he felt ecstatic. The angels (*phahomana*) were taking him on a heavenly journey to confront the lord of the sky and receive from him the words of truth, the secrets, and prophecies. Then he came down from the mountain and was expected to carry out the orders of his lord. This was exactly like what happened hundreds of years later with Muhammad at

---

Israa when he took a "spiritual and physical night journey" (called night of power).[101]

Zaradasht believed in judgment—a reward and
a punishment—and said that the spirit was created
before the physical body. His religion was created to
worship god and refuse the devil. Virtue was to be pro-
moted; vices and evil were to be avoided. He said that
god is the creator of the light and darkness. Zoroastrianism is essentially a doctrine of monotheism.

These beliefs and teachings were presented in the
first century BC in Persia. Islam advocated them, which
prompted Ali and Omar (the second and third caliphs
or princes of Islam after Muhammad) to respect Zaradasht and treat his followers just like the people of the
Bible (the book of Jews and Christians).[102]

SABIANISM

The Sabians were a monotheistic religious group. A
Sabian was someone who had left his faith. They were
divided into two groups: monotheists and infidels. The
Sabians worshiped the seven planets and believed in
the guidance of the stars. Many believers in Sabianism
were famous philosophers like Hilal bin Mohsen.[103]

---

[101] Sura 17

[102] موسوعة الأديان القديمة . معتقدات أسيوية . د / كامل سعفان ص
102_ 109

[103] مفاتيح الغيب أو التفسير الكبير ، فخر الدين الرازي تفسيره للآية
62من سورة البقرة

Muslim Arab scholars agree that the meaning of Sabianism can change depending on the situation, but some western scholars believe it means immersion or baptism.

Sabians taught that one must pray five times a day (just like the Muslims) toward the Kaaba. During Ramadan, they fasted and washed themselves of impurities if they touched a dead person or after sexual contact; and they avoided drinking alcohol, eating pork and some fowl, and eating anything found dead or with blood in it.[104]

Those who practiced Sabianism were forbidden to have sexual relations with a relative (just as Islam forbids). They were circumcised and married to only one wife in front of approved witnesses. The Quran says:

Indeed Allah will indeed judge between the faithful, the Jews, the Sabians, the Christians, the Magi, and the polytheists on the day of resurrection.[105]

They practiced meditation and drew closer to god through intercession with spiritual beings like angels:

Who is it that may intercede with him except with his permission?[106]

[104] الملل و النحل ج 1 فصل عبادة الصابئون و هياكلهم
قريش من القبيلة للدولة المركزية من ص205 إلى ص 222

[105] Sura 2:62, Sura 22:17

[106] Sura 2:55

As part of their rituals, they cut off the right hand of a thief, punished a murderer, and made the adulterer atone for his actions through stoning.[107]

ATHEIST BABYLONIAN RELIGION

The Babylonians worshiped the sun, but preferred to worship the moon because they believed it guided them. They worshiped the moon as the wise, the honest, the fair, the blessed, the appointed, the holy, and the protector, exactly like the attributes of Allah in Islam. They walked and followed the movement of the moon. Islam followed suit by counting and determining the days and months according to the movement of the moon.[108]

Worshipers of the sun, the moon, and the planets considered the sun as one of the angels; they believed it had a spirit and a mind, and that it was the source of light for the moon and the planets.

Anyone who did not believe in the end of days and the resurrection (life after death) was considered to be an infidel.[109]

They believed the devil could enter an idol and communicate through it or through the priest of an

---

الملل و النحل ج 1 فصل عبادة الصابئون و هياكلهم [107]

تاريخ العرب في عصر الجاهلية ـ ص462 , 463 [108]

بلوغ الأرب ج 2 ص 228 [109]

idol to foretell matters unseen. Some said it was the devil, while others said it was an angel.[110]

SUMMARY

As you have read, these religions all came before Islam, and some taught many good concepts, such as praying and fasting and pilgrimage to a holy land. They lived together in community and peace. None of these groups attacked each other or demanded the other to convert to their doctrines. They gave freedom of religion.

When Islam was born, years later, it stole the beliefs of these religions and claimed they were from Allah. Muhammad even had the audacity to tell people they must convert to Islam or die.

He took the prayers five times per day and the fasting from the Sabians. And just like Zaradasht took a heavenly journey to the top of a mountain to receive words of truth from the lord of the sky, Muhammad claimed to have met with an angel to receive words from Allah. From the monotheistic religions, Muhammad was inspired to do good things and not eat pork or drink wine.

Knowing all this, I ask, what new ethics did Islam give to its people?

بلوغ الأرب ج 2 ص 217 [110]

6

KAABAT IN THE ARABIAN PENINSULA AND ANCIENT WORLD

The society of the Arabian Peninsula consisted of groups of tribes that were scattered across the region and were ruled by the tribal norms. The elders and war heroes of the tribes became holy after their deaths. Their successors built statues in their honor and put them into temples, so they could be taken out for the people to seek their help and assistance in hard times.

Special worship customs began in order for the people to get closer to these holy dead ones, better known as lords (masters of the family or tribe). Special cubed houses (favored shape during this era), called *Kaabat* (or "houses of god"), were built for these worship customs.[111]

الإسلاميات . سيد القمني . ص19 [111]

All of the Kaabat (singular Kaaba) were built using holy, exotic, and rare stones such as volcanic and meteorite stones, most of which were black and strangely shaped as a result of combustion. The stones were considered sacred because of their shape and the fact that they were from an unknown metaphysical world.

Each stone came out of the ground due to volcanic eruptions, and according to the legend, was thought to contain the spirit of the holy ancestors.[112]

Meteorites were considered to have more dignity because they were dropped from the throne of god, with shining lights. So it was common for them to be surrounded with honor and veneration.

With the massive number of stones that had descended from the sky, representing the ancestors, the number of Kaabat being built increased. People took pilgrimages to these Kaabat thinking they were visiting god in his own house.

After Islam began, the twenty-one Kaabat that had been built in the Arabian Peninsula before Islam continued to be sanctified and visited in Mecca.[113]

Karen Armstrong wrote that the Arabs considered the Kaaba in Mecca to be a holy place to visit and practiced ancient rituals there based on their tribal lords.

---

112 الإسلاميات . سيد القمني . قصة الحضارات عصر الإيمان ان ص
١٨

113 الجذور التاريخية للشريعة الإسلامية . سيد القمني . ص65،22،21

This particular Kaaba was made famous because of its defeat of the Ethiopian elephant attack and because of the international markets that allowed the tribes access with their own idols.

Seven of the Kaabat were named after the planets: Sun, Moon, Jupiter, Saturn, Mars, Aurania (Uranus), and Venus. The most famous was called the "Sacred House." The people of Mecca were so proud of this Sacred House, they visited it during certain holy months (months without fighting) to worship and offer sacrifices to idols (fire stones). They kept this place clean and protected, especially during the Okaz Market (open air market).

Four months are considered holy, and the pilgrimage of Islam takes place in these months.[114]

The first person to put the holy statue of the god Hubal inside the Kaaba was Amr ibn Lahy, a leader of the Quraysh tribe. Others such as Essaf and Naaela followed Lahy. This sacred house was rebuilt ten times.

There were special legislations and rituals inside the Kaaba of Mecca, which were difficult to abide by. These included no fighting, no harming refugees who sought protection, and providing money to help host pilgrims. During the special Hajj pilgrimage to Mecca it was customary to stone the idol of Satan, and when they walked around the Kaaba seven times, they would say the words:

---

114 الألوسي . تاريخ الارب . ج3 ص78ـ المسعودي ج 2 ص 209

"For you, O god, I came here to obey you. You are the only god and there is no other but you."[115]

When Islam came, it kept these customs and called them traditions, even though these rituals came from infidels.

SUMMARY

If these people were in fact infidels, then how is it that they would know and practice the customs from Allah? If these people were infidels, then why would Muhammad accept their traditions as from Allah?

7

THE HISTORICAL
ROOTS OF SOME
ISLAMIC RITUALS

As previously mentioned, there were a lot of religions in the pre-Islamic Arabian Peninsula, including monotheism (Judaism and Nasraniah (false Christianity)), which had the greatest impact in forming the rules and regulations of the legislation of that era. Punishment and reward, stoning the adulterer, and other laws like cutting off the hands of thieves were all approved and adopted by Islam.

The name of Allah was familiar among the Arabs before Muhammad. In fact, Muhammad's father was named Abdullah, which means "servant of Allah." If Arabs did not believe or know about Allah before Muhammad, then why was his father's name Abdullah?

Islam consists of five pillars:

1. *Testifying that there is one god, Allah, and that Muhammad is his prophet*
2. *Paying tithes*
3. *Praying*
4. *Fasting during Ramadan*
5. *Journeying for pilgrimage (Hajj)*

If we prove that these five pillars were already part of the Arab tribal customs before Islam, then we need to ask of Muhammad, what new thing did he add? Because when Jesus Christ died on the cross, He said, "It is finished."

HAJJ PILGRIMAGE
(MOST IMPORTANT PILLAR OF ISLAM)

The religious practice of the Hajj pilgrimage during the month of Shawwal, month of Zu Alqeda, and ten days of Zu Alhija, was adopted into Islam.

The Arabs practiced certain rituals to honor their gods. The pilgrims would shave their heads and start the pilgrimage by circling around the house seven times in the direction of the sun. Then they visited the holy shrines to clean and kiss the Black Stone.[116]

مروج الذهب و معادن الجوهر . المسعودي . ج 2 ص208 [116]

They also used to go to the well of Zamzam to drink from it. Zamzam is thought to be the place where Hagar's son Ishmael drank.

Omar ibn al-Khattab (the second caliph) said in front of the Black Stone: "I definitely know that you are a useless stone and I would have never done that unless I saw the messenger of Allah kissing you."[117]

Muslims would travel back and forth between Safa and Marwa (two small hills located in Mecca) seven times during the Hajj pilgrimage.

One ritual the Arabs followed was to stand on Mount Arafah (Mount Arafat), the second holy place on the pilgrimage, and slaughter an animal while raising their voices in song as they were purified. They did not wear any clothing made of wool during the pilgrimage and used the same phrases and calls that Muslims use today.[118]

Muhammad claimed that Allah ordered him to establish special rituals in Islam for the pilgrimage; however, his rituals were the same that were already in existence from the Arabs before his time. Dr. Abdul-Rahman Badawi (Egyptian poet and existentialist professor of philosophy) confirmed that Islam

---

دفاع عن محمد ضد منتقصيه ص174 [117]

[118] اليعقوبي ج1 ص254 ـ356 ، بلوغ الأرب في معرفة أحوال العرب . ج2 ص196و 230 و288 سيرة أبن هشام ج1 ص53، سيرة النبي محمد . كارين أرمسترونچ ص96 ـ100

revived and approved these rituals for the pilgrimage, with some amendments.[119]

The Hajj pilgrimage is one of the most important pillars of Islam. If Muslim authors have confirmed that this was already in place before Islam came to Muhammad, what new thing does Islam offer?

THE FASTING OF RAMADAN (SECOND PILLAR OF ISLAM)

The Sabians taught the necessity of fasting during the month of Ramadan (the new moon), and praying facing the Kaaba to magnify it.[120]

It was forbidden to eat anything found dead or with blood. Muslims would fast for twenty-nine to thirty days, according to the moon. Dr. Abdul-Rahman Badawi said that the fasting of Ramadan was present before Islam on Arabian Peninsula.[121]

Muhammad, during his stay in Mecca, kept this ritual during his time. After his migration to Yathrib during Shabaan (Arab calendar months in the second year of migration), he ordered the fasting of Ramadan:

O you who have faith! Prescribed for you is fasting as it was prescribed for those who were

---

دفاع عن محمد ضد المنتقصين من قدره . ص171 [119]

بلوغ الأرب في معرفة . العرب.ج2 . 224 [120]

دفاع عن محمد ضد المنتقصين من قدره . د/ عبد الرحمن بدوي ص [121]
166 ,169

before you, so that you may be godwary.[122]

Dr. Badawi writes that a group of Manichaean (religious sect taught Mani) fasted for thirty days according to the path of the moon, and also the al-Haranin fasted for thirty days starting at Azar to glorify the moon.

If fasting is one of the pillars of Islam and it was in place long before Islam started, then what is the point of Islam?

PRAYERS
(THIRD PILLAR OF ISLAM)

The believers in the Sabian religion prayed five prayers at night and during the day. Also, the Manichaean sect in Mesopotamia called for four prayers at night and during the day. When Islam came, five obligatory prayers were said at night and during the day, including praying for the dead without bowing or prostrating oneself. Islam follows the same prayer ritual as the Sabians—same ways (washing before prayer; and stand, bow, and kneel) and same times.[123]

Dr. Badawi says that nothing is mentioned in the Quran stating the imposition of the five daily prayers. But the Quran does command prayer at four different times:

---

[122] Sura 2:183, 185

[123] بلوغ الأرب في معرفة أحوال العرب . ج2 . 224_ معتقدات
أسيوية .موسوعة الأديان ص140

1. *And establish prayers at the two ends of the day and the first hours of night.*[124]

2. *Establish prayer at the decline of the sun until the darkness of the night.*[125]

3. *Maintain with care the prayers and in particular the middle.*[126]

Muslim commentators offer little explanation as to why there are only four prayers mentioned here:

> *So exalted is Allah when you reach the evening and when you reach the morning, and to him is praise throughout the heaven and the earth, and at night and when you are at noon.*[127]

In these verses we find it crucial and conclusive to pray, but without any clear guidelines as to when or how often.

AL-HEDOD (SHARIA LAW)

Hedod means *Sharia,* and pertains to the religious law or rules. As Moses received rules from God to organize and judge the children of Israel, Muhammad said that he also received rules from Allah to govern the people. Because this is a holy law, people must respect it. How-

---

[124] Sura 11:114

[125] Sura 17:78

[126] Sura 2:238

[127] Sura 30:17-18

ever, we will discover that the holy law in Islam did not come down by revelation from heaven, but rather grew up from the Arabian Peninsula.

As you read this section, consider: If the holy Muslim rules were founded before Islam, then what is the need for Islam? As we have learned, the pillars of Islam were already in place before Muhammad's inspiration.

Defamation or Accusations of One's Ancestry

The ancestry of the Arab man was very important to his status and pride. The worst thing to say about an old Arab was that he was not attributed to his father or that his pedigree was unknown, thus defaming his character. Anyone who said these things (curses) was punished with eighty lashes.

Islam borrowed this from the ancient Arabs:

And those who accuse chaste women and then do not produce four witnesses, lash them with eighty lashes and do not accept from them testimony even after, and those are the defiantly disobedient.[128]

Thievery

To punish a thief, Arabs used to cut off the right hand of a thief after he stole something.[129] Walid ibn al-Mugh-

---

[128] Sura 24:4

الإسلام بين الدولة الدينية و المدنية ص153

بلوغ الأرب في معرفة أحوال العرب . ج2 ص292 [129]

irah was the first to practice this, because he was a butcher and was afraid slaves would steal his money.

When Muhammad was thirty-five years old, someone stole a treasure from the Kaaba. The man was from the Arabian tribe Banu Amr ibn Aif. The Quraysh cut off his hand. This is now known as a famous incident in Islam.[130]

If al-Mughirah formed this judgment by himself before Muhammad, and Muhammad confirmed this law, then should we not also accept al-Mughirah as a prophet?

Thievery on the Roads

The kings of Yemen and al-Hirah crucified any man (outlaw) who plundered people along the road, violating the boundary lines.[131]

There is a story told by Muslims that says that Islam adopted this law. Abu Nasr Ahmed (a vizier) said that a group (30-70 people) from the tribes of Akl and Orina came to the messenger of Allah (Muhammad) and said: "O messenger of Allah, we are the people of the udder not the people of the countryside and now we live in the city (Yathrib)." Then the messenger of Allah ordered them to drink the milk and pee of female

الإسلام بين الدولة الدينية و الدولة المدنية . خليل عبد الكريم . ص 152 [130]

سيرة أبن هشام ج1 ص122

بلوغ الأرب في معرفة أحوال العرب . ج 2 ص292 [131]

camels (not less than three and not more than thirty). But the shepherd of the camels was killed.

Abu Qatada (a scholar of the Quran) said that those who fight Allah and his messenger and spread mischief on earth are to be punished.[132] The Quran instructs:

> *Those who wage war against Allah and his messenger, and go about the earth spreading mischief – indeed their recompense is that they either be done to death, or be crucified, or have their hands and feet cut off from the opposite sides, or be banished from the land. Such will be their degradation in the world, and in the hereafter theirs will be an awful doom.[133]*

The story continues to say that Muhammad cut off their hands and feet, plucked out their eyes, and crucified them.[134]

In the Old Testament, two men from the tribe of Benjamin killed Ish-bosheth (the son of King Saul) while he was sleeping and cut off his head. They went to David to brag that they had killed the son of his enemy. But the Bible says:

ص ١٣٠ النيسابوري أسباب النزول [132]

[133] Sura 5:33

رواه مسلم في صحيحه . كتاب٣ الديات و المحاربين و القسامة١٦٢ [134]

And David commanded his young men, and
they killed them and cut off their hands and feet
and hanged them beside the pool at Hebron.[135]

There is a great difference between the violence
in the Old Testament and the violence of Islam. David
commanded these two men to be killed because they
took an innocent life. Muhammad took his judgment
of thievery to the extreme. In fact, Muhammad took
this one time command of David and created a law
with it, making this practice the norm in Islam.

SOCIAL RITUALS

Just as Abd al-Muttalib paid the purchase price of one
hundred camels in exchange for his youngest son's life,
the Arabs also used the price of camels as blood money.

Imam Malik, a great teacher of Islam, wrote that,
according to the prophet's message to Amr bin Hazm,
the blood money for a man was one hundred camels; for
an eye, hand, or leg, it was fifty camels; for each finger, it
was ten camels; yet for a tooth, it was five camels. This
same story has been confirmed by al-Darami.[136]

Marriage and Divorce

Arabs have different kinds of marriage rituals.
When Muhammad came, he approved all of their mar-

---

[135] 2 Samuel 4:12

سنن الدارمي . كتاب الديات ٢٢٥٩. [136]

riages. Before they were married, the groom would go to the bride's family and pay a price, or dowry, for his bride. This is the most common of all marriage rituals.

A *mut'ah* marriage was a temporary marriage. This came about when Arab men would travel or go to war. While away from their families, they would pay money to a woman to be temporarily married to her.[137]

Before Islam, Arabs were allowed to divorce and remarry the same woman up to three times. However, after the third time they were forbidden to marry the same person again.

In the Arabian Peninsula, it was forbidden to marry one's aunt, father's wife, or sisters.[138]

We see here how Judaism influenced the Arabs in their marriage rules and rituals. Because they were "people of the book" (Judaism and Nasraniah), the curse for breaking this law was known. The Arab law was taken directly from the Bible:

> *"'Cursed be anyone who lies with his father's wife, because he has uncovered his father's nakedness.' And all the people shall say, 'Amen.' 'Cursed be anyone who lies with any kind of animal.' And all the people shall say, 'Amen.' 'Cursed be anyone who lies with his*

بلوغ الارب في معرفة أحوال العرب ج٢ ص٢٩٢ [137]

المرجع السابق ج 2 ص 52 ـ تاريخ العرب في عصر الجاهلية .ص [138] 446 و447

*sister, whether the daughter of his father or
the daughter of his mother.' And all the people
shall say, 'Amen.' 'Cursed be anyone who lies
with his mother-in-law.' And all the people
shall say, 'Amen.'"*[139]

Prohibition of Alcohol and Female Infanticide

The prohibition of adultery, drinking alcohol, gambling, and female infanticide started in the Jewish law:

*And the LORD spoke to Aaron, saying, "Drink
no wine or strong drink, you or your sons
with you, when you go into the tent of meeting, lest you die. It shall be a statute forever
throughout your generations."*[140]

Adullah Abu al-Qasim al-Saadi wrote a book in 555
AD called *The Disadvantages of Wine.* Afif bin Moad, the
uncle of al-Ashat, wrote poems on that subject as well.
Aisha, Muhammad's wife, said that Abu Bakr (Aisha's
father and Muhammad's close friend) never drank
alcohol, and neither did Othman (Aisha's cousin and
Muhammad's close friend). Zaradasht called for the
prohibition of drinking alcohol because it desecrated
the body and the mind. He also prohibited adultery,
lying, and murder. Al-Saban did not permit the eating

[139] Deuteronomy 27:20-23
[140] Leviticus 10:8-9

of anything found dead or with blood, the eating of any pork, or the drinking of wine.[141]

Abd al-Muttalib, Muhammad's grandfather, forbade the drinking of wine and the killing of infant daughters. It was a legend that sons were more valuable than daughters, so when a girl was born to an Arab family, they would dispose of her; but they would keep all boys.[142]

We see that Abu Bakr, father of Aisha and the first caliph; Othman, the third caliph; and Abd al-Muttalib abstained from drinking wine before Islam. They also never allowed female infanticide before Islam. These men were very close to Muhammad and they forbade these practices. So, who influenced whom? What new thing did Muhammad bring in forbidding wine and female infanticide?

If the Arabs of the Arabian Peninsula killed infant girls before Islam, then why did Abu Bakr keep his daughter, Aisha (Muhammad's child wife)? Muhammad's first wife, Khadija, was a very influential woman. She owned a business and was very wealthy. If the Arabs did indeed kill all of the girls at birth, then how would they be able to reproduce?

[141] بلوغ الأرب في معرفة أحوال العرب . ج2 . 224 و294 و296_
موسوعة الأديان القديمة . معتقدات آسيوية ص104

[142] تاريخ اليعقوبي ج 2 ص10

Dogs are Unclean

In Islam, dogs are considered impure, according to some Hadiths and Sunnahs. This comes from the Jewish law:

> *You shall not bring the fee of a prostitute or the wages of a dog into the house of the LORD your God in payment for any vow, for both of these are an abomination to the LORD your God.*[143]

The same meaning of the dog being impure is also seen in the Hadith, as mentioned by Muhammad.[144]

Take Off Shoes on Holy Ground

In Islam, it is considered offensive if one enters a holy place wearing shoes. Therefore, Allah ordered people to take off their shoes before entering a mosque and during prayer, just like the former prophets Moses and Abraham did. This was sacred to the Jews, especially in places where the Angel of the Lord appeared to the prophets and the men of God at that time. Examples of this are seen in the Old Testament with Moses and Joshua.

> *And the angel of the LORD appeared to him in a flame of fire out of the midst of a bush.*

---

[143] Deuteronomy 23:18

[144] مسلم كتاب السقاة رقم2932

He looked, and behold, the bush was burning, yet it was not consumed. And Moses said, "I will turn aside to see this great sight, why the bush is not burned." When the LORD saw that he turned aside to see, God called to him out of the bush, "Moses, Moses!" And he said "Here I am." Then he said, "Do not come near; take your sandals off your feet, for the place on which you are standing is holy ground."[145]

We see another example in Joshua:

And the commander of the LORD's army said to Joshua, "Take off your sandals from your feet, for the place where you are standing is holy." And Joshua did so.[146]

After Islam came, this principle was stressed, especially in prayer, and we know that the removing of shoes in holy places became a known doctrine.

From the smallest detail, like the removal of shoes for prayer and the touching of dogs, to the largest detail, Islam brought nothing new. These things were already in place before its time.

---

[145] Exodus 3:2-5

[146] Joshua 5:15

Usury

Jewish law forbids usury:

> *"You shall not charge interest on loans to your brother, interest on money, interest on food, interest on anything that is lent for interest. You may charge a foreigner interest, but you may not charge your brother interest, that the LORD your God may bless you in all that you undertake in the land that you are entering to take possession of it."*[147]

As a result of the respected law, the Arabs, especially the Hanafi, forbade usury as well:

> *But Allah has permitted trade and has forbidden the interest.*[148]

Muhammad, through his Hadith, cursed anyone who demanded usury.[149]

Holy Months

Klab bin Mara was the first to give specific names to the months and a reason for each one, starting with Muharram, because it is the beginning of the year. Four of the twelve months are considered sacred: Rajab *(request, honor)*, Dhu al-Qa'dah *(the one of truce/settling)*,

---

[147] Deuteronomy 23:19-20

[148] Sura 2:275

[149] سنن الدارمي كتاب البيوع 2423

Dhu al-Hijjah *(the one of pilgrimage),* and Muharram *(forbidden to kill).* Hajj months are: Shawwal, Zu al-Qeda, and ten days of Zu al-Hija. These are exactly the same as the Islamic months.[150]

During the sacred months, it was forbidden to take revenge on the killer of one's father or brother; it was normal for two people who had been fighting to reconcile. The Quran says:

> *Indeed, the number of numbers with Allah is twelve months in the register of Allah from the day he created the heavens and the earth; of these, four are sacred. This is the correct religion, so don't wrong yourselves during them. And fight against the disbelievers collectively as they fight against you collectively. And know that Allah is with the righteous.[151]*

The fast of Ashura was held on the tenth of Muharram (Arabic calendar months) and the first of Rajab. In ignorance, the Quraysh fasted during this time. It is said that the Quraysh committed a sin, and the fast was done to purge the sin. This day became sacred and the Kaaba was covered. Another thought is that the people suffered a drought but survived, so they fasted in thanksgiving.[152]

---

[150] بلوغ الأرب في معرفة أحوال العرب . ج3   ص79

[151] Sura 9:36

[152] بلوغ الأرب في معرفة أحوال العرب . ج2   ص288

Prior to giving his prophecy, Muhammad also fasted during Ashura. After he migrated to Yathrib, he kept fasting and ordered others to fast as well. When the imposition of fasting during the month of Ramadan was implemented, he said about Ashura, "Who wants to fast it [Ashura]…it doesn't matter."[153]

As for fasting on the first of Rajab, Muhammad did this before and after his migration. No one knows why the first of Rajab was considered holy; however, one of the customs during that day was to reconcile differences between each other.[154]

The ancient Arabs named the days of the week starting with Sunday, because it is the first day that God created. The others also have meaning—Monday (al-Ethnen) means the second day; Tuesday means the third day; Wednesday means the fourth day; Thursday means the fifth day; Friday means the gathering day; Saturday means the day of rest.

The Jews' holy day was Saturday; the Nasraniah holy day was Sunday. The Arabs decided to meet together the day before both of them because they wanted to be first. They gathered together on Friday, the gathering day. They met together and prayed together, bowing twice, exactly as Muslims do today in their prayers. The Quran says:

---

[153] صحيح مسلم كتاب الصيام رقم1897

[154] بلوغ الأرب في معرفة أحوال العرب ج3 ص 79

O ye who believe! When the call is proclaimed to prayer on Friday (the Day of Assembly), hasten earnestly to the remembrance of Allah, and leave off business (and traffic): That is best for you if ye but knew![155]

On Fridays, the Quraysh met together, listened to a leader preach, and prayed together, similar to the Nasraniah practice on Sundays.[156]

If the Jews gathered for worship on the Sabbath to remember God created the world in six days and rested on the seventh day, and if the Christians worshiped on Sundays to commemorate the resurrection of Christ, what made Muslims gather on Friday? Do they imitate the people of the book? If they do, they did not choose the day that the Lord made holy, but the day that the Arabs of ignorance chose!

Eating and Drinking

When it came to food, the Arabs did not fill their stomachs. "Full stomach let acumen go!" Muhammad preached that while Muslims ate, they should leave one-third of their stomach for food, one-third for drink, and one-third to breathe. A Hadith says: "When

---

[155] Sura 62:9-11

بلوغ الإرب . ج 1 ص 273ـ ج 2 ص 282

[156] تفسير ابن كثير لسورة الجمعة ايه٩

بلوغ الإرب . ج1 ص273 ـ ج2 ص282

you drink water, suck it and do not fill your stomach because it hurts your liver."

They believed that too much food would spoil the mind. Luqman (a wise man like Solomon) said: "My son, if stomach is full, ideas sleep, wisdom is shut up, and organs can not worship."[157]

Jews did not eat pork, as they considered it unclean:

"And the pig, because it parts the hoof but does not chew the cud, is unclean for you. Their flesh you shall not eat, and their carcasses you shall not touch."[158]

This belief was also held to in Al-Ahnaf and Islam:

Prohibited to you are dead animals, blood, and the flesh of swine.[159]

As for drinking, the Arabs preferred to sit down while drinking, and they followed the custom of drinking three sips, not one. When Islam came, it followed this ritual exactly.

Among the kings of the Arabian Peninsula, it was preferred to use the right hand for drinking and for everything else. The Arabs used to imitate their kings in this habit, and when Islam came, this habit did not change. It was tradition in their day to honor the right

---

بلوغ الأرب في معرفة أحوال العرب ج1 ص 378 و388 [157]

[158] Deuteronomy 14:8

[159] Sura 5:3

hand over the left hand. Any honored guests would sit to the right hand of the host.[160]

The Quran says:

> *But consider who will introduce his book – in the day of judgment – with the right hand is of the people of paradise, and who will introduce his book with the left hand is of the people of hell.[161]*

Angels and Demons

Angels and demons play a role in one particular sect of the Arab religion, which believed that the good doer was the light and the evildoer was the dark. Light gave birth to angels; while darkness gave birth to demons. They believed that the angels were helping us to do well, and demons were preventing us from doing good.[162]

Many people believed that a priest was required to have a relationship with the devil to tell the people what they missed. When the devil heard the news, he would then inform the priest, who then delivered the message to the listener. When the Quran came, it supported this idea:

---

[160] بلوغ الأرب في معرفة أحوال العرب ج1 ص394

[161] Sura 69:19

[162] بلوغ الأرب .ج2 ص230

And indeed do the devils inspire their allies to dispute with you.[163]

The Ritual of Stoning

The ritual of stoning was an essential rite of pilgrimage before Islam. In Taif (city in Mecca), the tribe of Thaqif (a tribe near Mecca) sent Abu Rghal to guide the King of Ethiopia, Abraha, on the road to demolish the Kaaba. On the way, in al-Maghmas, Abu Rghal died. Because of his death on the way to destroy the Kaaba, the Arabs thought he betrayed them and they stoned his tomb. On the road between Taif and Mecca lies the tomb of Abu Rghal. To this day, Arabs throw stones at it.[164]

In his historical book, ibn Hashim explains that during their pilgrimage, Arabs would stand on Mount Arafat and throw stones. The most famous Arab tribe, Suffa, honored this ritual long before Islam.[165]

The Quran says that Hagar, the wife of Abraham, stoned the devil when he wanted to whisper to her. Islam approved this ritual, whether because of the stoning of the tomb of Abu Rghal or the stoning of the devil at the Black Stone.

---

[163] Sura 6:121

بلوغ الأرب ج 2 ص177

[164] د/ السيد عبد العزيز سالم . تاريخ العرب في العصر الجاهلي ص

166 ـ المسعودي مروج الذهب و ج 2 ص86ص 86

[165] ابن هشام ج١ ص٧٨

Adultery

Among the Jews, the law of stoning the adulterer and the adulteress is seen in the Torah:

> *If there is a betrothed virgin, and a man meets her in the city and lies with her, then you shall bring them both out to the gate of that city, and you shall stone them to death with stones, the young woman because she did not cry for help though she was in the city, and the man because he violated his neighbor's wife. So you shall purge the evil from your midst.*[166]

Islam held to this same law:

> *And we ordained for them therein a life for a life, an eye for an eye, a nose for a nose, an ear for an ear, a tooth for a tooth, and for wounds is legal retribution.*[167]

Prohibition of Likening Women to Men and Vice Versa

The Jewish law forbade women to imitate men and men to imitate women:

> *A woman shall not wear a man's garment, nor shall a man put on a woman's cloak, for who-*

---

[166] Deuteronomy 22:23-24

[167] Sura 5:45

ever does these things is an abomination to the LORD your God.[168]

Likewise, Muhammad said:

Allah has cursed men who imitate women, and women who imitate men.[169]

Treatment for the Poor, Wayfarers, Orphans and Widows

Before Islam, Al-Ahnaf commanded the care of the poor, wayfarers, orphans, and widows. This teaching is found in the Bible:

"When you reap your harvest in your field and forget a sheaf in the field, you shall not go back to get it. It shall be for the sojourner, the fatherless, and the widow, that the LORD your God may bless you in all the work of your hands."[170]

"'Cursed be anyone who perverts the justice due to the sojourner, the fatherless, and the widow.' And all the people shall say, 'Amen.'"[171]

---

[168] Deuteronomy 22:5

[169] Sahih al-Bukhari, Book of Dress, 77, Hadith 102

[170] Deuteronomy 24:19

[171] Deuteronomy 27:19
مروج الذهب ج2 ص138
موسوعة الأديان القديمة . معتقدات آسيوية . ص106

Muslims give us the idea that before Islam, the Arabs did not support the oppressed and did not keep their promises or respect their vows. But Arabic writers, like ibn Hashim, said that the Arabs were famous for their hospitality and kindness to the oppressed. They would light fires around their homes at night to light the way for anyone lost and welcome them into their homes.[172]

In Deuteronomy 23:21, God gave orders for the Jews to respect their vows. The impression Islam gives us about the Arab people in this day is wrong.

Life after Death

Poetry and linguistics affected the way the Quran was written. The flowery rhetoric was used in the Arabian Peninsula—specifically words like *baath (resurrection), reward, punishment,* and *the one god.* The names used to refer to god—holy, sincere, wise, blessed, appointed, and protector—were known especially in Mesopotamia. The Arab people believed in the resurrection, meaning life after death. The good would be in paradise and the bad would be in hell. This teaching was from Zaradasht and came before Islam.[173]

Islam used the same teaching as Zaradasht, Judiasm, and Nasraniah regarding life after death.

أبن هشام ج1 ص 87 [172]
اليعقوبي ج1 ص254 و258 ج2 ص18

مروج الذهب ج2 ص138 [173]
موسوعة الأديان القديمة . معتقدات آسيوية . ص106

WAR RITUALS OF ISLAM

When an Arab tribe would conquer another, the leader of the tribe would take for himself the best of the spoils before dividing the remaining amongst his army. When Islam came, Muhammad used this rite for himself. He took Safeya as his slave, and later (after she converted to Islam), he married her.[174]

Abu Dawood wrote that before Muhammad divided the spoils of war among his people, he would choose something for himself. That might be a horse, salt, or a slave.[175]

Fourth of Booty

Before Islam, the leader of an Arab tribe, after conquering another tribe, would take one-fourth of the booty. Muhammad kept this same rule in Islam but said one-fifth was for himself. The Quran teaches:

> *And know that out of all booty that ye may acquire (in war), a fifth share is assigned to Allah, and to the messenger.*[176]

As you can see here, Allah of Islam commanded the same rule of spoils as what was traditional in the Arab

---

[174] الجذور التاريخية للشريعة الإسلامية . خليل عبد الكريم ص99، 100

ـ تاريخ العرب في العصر الجاهلي . ص4 ، 15

[175] سننه في كتاب الخراج و الإمارة رقم2597

[176] Sura 8:41
تاريخ العرب في العصر الجاهلي . ص415

tribes previously. Before, the leader would keep one-fourth of the spoils for himself and divide the other three-fourths among his army. Muhammad took this rule and changed it to one-fifth for himself, and for the other four-fifths, he wrote an order as to how it was to be divided. In the Quran, we read:

> *A fifth share is assigned to Allah, and to the messenger, and to near relatives, orphans, the needy, and the wayfarer, if ye do believe in Allah and in the revelation we sent down to our servant on the Day of Testin, the day of the meeting of the two forces. For Allah hath power over all things.*[177]

Looting

The custom in the early Arab tribes during a raid was for the soldier who killed another to be eligible to take the deceased's goods, whether they be armor, horse, clothes, or weapons. This tradition was brought without modification into Islamic law.

Tirmidhi (Hadith writer) wrote in his book that Muhammad gave permission for Muslims to kill any non-Muslim and take their possessions:

> *Auf bin Malik (RAA) narrated, "The messenger of Allah judged that the belongings taken*

---

[177] Sura 8:41

*from the (non-Muslim enemy) killed sol-
dier in a war, are to be given to the one who
killed him."*[178]

What is different between Allah's rules in the
battle and the infidel's battle rules? If these people
were infidels and did not have ethics as Muhammad
claimed, then why did Allah take their rules and adapt
them as his own?

SUMMARY

Islam built five pillars: followers must (1) testify
that Allah was the only god and Muhammad was his
prophet; (2) pay Zakaat (tithes or offerings); (3) pray
five times per day; (4) fast Ramadan; and (5) journey
for Hajj. We have discovered in these chapters the
roots to all these pillars. Do you think these pillars
came from heaven or from culture?

Regarding Sharia Law, we know that Islam has rules
and punishments for breaking these rules, all of which
already existed in pre-Islamic times. For instance, the
punishment for thievery is to cut off the hand, and blood
money (the price of 100 camels) must be paid when a
person murders another. Even the holy months written
about in the Quran were found in the pre-Islamic days.
What did Islam bring to the Arab culture that was new?

---

[178] Sahih Muslims Book 44, Hadith 1753
الترمذي بكتاب السير رقم2345

Conclusion

There are still several issues regarding the pre-Islamic Arabian Peninsula that could have been covered in this book. These would have helped to even further expose their religious background and shed light on what Islam had inherited from these ancient religions, and would have demonstrated even more the great impact of Judaism and Christianity on the Arabic community—then and now. The impact has been felt across worship practices, principles, and customs, which then led to Islam. The rituals and laws that they instituted as a result show how the ancient community moved over to Islam without barely even a single amendment to any of them.

Christian heresies, specifically Marianism and Nasraniah, negatively affected al-Hijaz. These also distorted the gospel and denied the divinity of Christ and His crucifixion.

The economic, cultural, and scientific backgrounds played an important role in moving culture from place

to place, disproving the false claims about the igno-rance and isolation of Arabs at that time. The truth of their excellence in medicine, mathematics, astronomy, and the sciences is proven.

For now, the true Islam has been revealed through original resources, holding them accountable.

Questions from the Author

Dear Reader,

Suppose you meet a writer who gives you a book and says, "I wrote this book. It is an original from me." Then you find several other books that have exactly the same details in them, and these books were written hundred of years prior. What would you call this writer? Could you trust him, especially when he not only claims that the previous authors of the same information were liars and infidels, but he also killed them for their misinformation?

Now that you have finished reading this book, you have seen that the Quran was written based on the culture of the Arabian Peninsula. In your opinion, do you think Islam came from heaven or from the Arab culture?

Brother K

TABLE OF SIMILARITIES

The following table shows the similarities between Islam and Judaism in a number of things already mentioned.

	ISLAM	JUDAISM
Monotheism	"And it was already revealed to you and to those before you that if you should associate anything with Allah, your work would surely become worthless, and you would surely be among the losers" *(39:65)*.	"Hear, O Israel: The LORD our God, the LORD is one" *(Deuteronomy 6:4)*.

	ISLAM	JUDAISM
Monotheism *(Continued)*	"Say, 'it is only revealed to me that your god is but one god;' so will be Muslims in submission to him?" *(21:108)*.	
Prohibition of Killing	"And do not kill the soul which Allah has forbidden except by right" *(17:33)*.	"Keep far from a false charge, and do not kill the innocent and righteous, for I will not acquit the wicked" *(Exodus 23:7)*.
Prohibition of Adultery	"And do not approach unlawful sexual intercourse. Indeed, it is ever an immorality and is evil as a way" *(17:32)*.	"You shall not commit adultery" *(Exodus 20:14)*.

	ISLAM	JUDAISM
Honoring Your Father and Mother	"And your lord has decreed that you not worship except him, and to parents, good treatment" *(17:23)*.	"Honor your father and your mother, that your days may be long in the land that the LORD your God is giving you" *(Exodus 20:12)*.
Caring for Orphans and the Needy	"And do not approach the orphan's property except in a way that is best" *(6:152)*. "So as for the orphan, do not oppress [him]" *(93:9)*.	"'Cursed be anyone who perverts the justice due to the sojourner, the fatherless, and the widow.' And all the people shall say, 'Amen.'" *(Deuteronomy 27:19)*.
Honest Scales	"And give full measure and weight in justice" *(6:152)*. "And establish weight in justice and do not make deficient the balance" *(55:9)*.	"You shall do no wrong in judgment, in measures of length or weight or quantity" *(Leviticus 19:35)*.

	ISLAM	JUDAISM
Prohibition of Idol Worship	"Oh you who believed, indeed, intoxicants, gambling [sacrificing on] stone alerts [to other than Allah]" *(5:90)*.	"You shall not make idols for yourselves or erect an image or pillar and you shall not set up a figured stone in your land to bow down to it, for I am the LORD your God" *(Leviticus 26:1)*.
Helping the Poor, Needy, and Stranger	"Zakah expenditures are only for the poor and for the needy" *(9:60)*. "And know that anything you obtain of war booty – then indeed, for Allah is one-fifth of it and for the messenger and for [his] near relatives and the orphans, the needy and the [stranded] traveler" *(8:41)*.	"For there will never cease to be poor in the land. Therefore I command you, You shall open wide your hand to your brother, to the needy, and to the poor, in your land" *(Deuteronomy 15:11)*.

	ISLAM	JUDAISM
Prohibition of Ridiculing Others	"O you who have believed, let not a people ridicule [another] people, perhaps they may be better than them" *(49:11)*.	"Condemnation is ready for scoffers, and beating for the backs of fools" *(Proverbs 19:29)*.
Prohibition of Incest	"Prohibited to you [for marriage] are your mothers, your daughters, your sisters, your father's sisters, your mother's sisters, your brother's daughters, your sister's daughters" *(4:23)*.	"None of you shall approach any one of his close relatives to uncover nakedness. I am the LORD" *(Leviticus 18:6)*.

	ISLAM	JUDAISM
Washing Before Prayer	"O you who have believed, when you rise to [perform] prayer, wash your faces and your forearms to the elbows and wipe over your heads and wash your feet to the ankles" *(5:6)*.	"With which Aaron and his sons shall wash their hands and their feet. When they go into the tent of meeting, or when they come near the altar to minister, to burn a food offering to the LORD, they shall wash with water, so that they may not die" *(Exodus 30:19-20)*.

RESOURCES AND REFERENCES

القرآن .

الكتاب المقدس) العهد القديم ـ الجديد(.

تفسير الجلالين .

تفسير القرآن لفخر الدين الرازي .

تفسير القرآن لأبن كثير . المكتبة التوفيقية .

تفسير القرطبي .

قصص الأنبياء لأبن كثير . تحقيق عصام الدين الصبابطي . طبعة دار الفجر بالأزهر .

أسباب النزول للسيوطي .

موسوعة الحديث الشريف . الكتب التسعة .

بلوغ الأرب في معرفة أحوال العرب . الألوسي . حققه
محمد بهجة الأثري . دار الكتب العلمية ـ بيروت .

تاريخ العرب في عصر الجاهلية . د/ سيد عبد العزيز
سالم . دار النهضة العربية ـ بيروت .

مروج الذهب و معادن الجوهر . المسعودي . تحقيق .
سهام محمد اللحام . دار الفكر . طبعة أولى .

السيرة النبوية ـ أبن هشام .تحقيق . الشيخ محمد
بيومي . المكتب الثقافي . الأزهر ـ القاهرة .

البداية و النهاية ـ أبن كثير ، دار الكتب العلمية ، طبعة
رابعة عام1988 بيروت .

أسد الغابة في معرفة أحوال الصحابة ـ عز الدين بن
الإثير . أبي الحسن علي بن محمد الجزري .

تاريخ اليعقوبي ـ أحمد بن يعقوب بن جعفر بن وهب .
دار صادر ـ بيروت .

طبقات الكبرى . محمد بن سعد ، دار صادر ـ بيروت .

الكامل التاريخ . إبن الأثير . تحقيق أبي الفداء عبد الله
القاضي . دار الكتب العلمية .بيروت

معجم البلدان. للشيخ الإمام شهاب الدين أبي عبد الله
ياقوت بن عبد الله الحموي . دار صادر بيروت.

تاريخ أبي الفداء المسمى المختصر في أخبار البشر .
تعليق . محمود ديوب . دار الكتب العلمية .لبنان

قريش من القبلية إلى الدولة المركزية ـ خليل عبد
الكريم . دار سينا . طبعة ثانية .

النص المؤسس و مجتمعه . السفر الأول و الثاني . خليل
عبد الكريم . دار مصر المحروسة.

الإسلام ما بين الدولة الدينية و الدولة المدنية . خليل عبد
الكريم . دار سيناء طبعة أولى .

الجذور التاريخية للشريعة الإسلامية . خليل عبد
الكريم . دار سينا . طبعة ثانية .

الحزب الهاشمي و تأسيس الدولة الإسلامية . سيد
محمود القمني . مدبولي الصغير . طبعة رابعة.

الأعمال الإسلاميات: قراءة اجتماعية سياسية للسيرة
النبوية . سيد القمني .

أحكام الزواج و الطلاق في الإسلام . الشيخ بدران .
دائرة المعارف الكتابية للكتاب المقدس .

تاريخ الفكر المسيحي . القس حنا الخضري .

تاريخ الكنيسة القبطية . القس منسى يوحنا .

المسيحية و الحضارة العربية . الأب د/ جورج شحاته
قنواتي . دار الثقافة . القاهرة .

موسوعة الأديان القديمة . قسم المعتقدات أسيوية . د/ كامل سعفان ـ دار الندى .

حكايات الدخول . هوامش الفتح العربي الإسلامي لمصر . سناء المصري . دار سيناء .

سيرة النبي محمد . كارين أرمسترونج . الطبعة الثانية . القاهرة .

دفاع عن محمد ضد المنتقصين من قدره . د/ عبد الرحمن بدوي . الدار العالمية للكتب و النشر .

The Ministry of ANM

*ANM Publications is a ministry initiative
of Advancing Native Missions*

Advancing Native Missions (ANM) is a U.S.-based Christian missions agency. However, unlike many such agencies that are involved in sending missionaries from America to other places around the world, ANM works with indigenous missionaries. Indigenous (or native) missionaries are Christian workers who minister within their own sphere of influence proclaiming the Gospel of Jesus Christ to their own people. ANM then works to connect Christians in America with these brothers and sisters, to equip and encourage them. Our goal is to build relationships of love and trust between indigenous missionaries and North American individuals and churches. In this way, the entire body of Christ becomes involved in completing the Great Commission. **"And this gospel of the kingdom shall be preached in all the world as a witness to all nations, and then the end shall come"** (Matthew 24:14).

If you would like to know how you can become an effective coworker with native missionaries to reach the unreached for Jesus Christ, contact ANM at contact@AdvancingNativeMissions.com, call us at 540-456-7111, or visit our website:

www.AdvancingNativeMissions.com